inside
25 cromwell st

stephen & mae west

Peter Grose Publishing

Published by
Peter Grose Ltd
Monmouth
in association with
News of the World
London

Copyright © News Group Newspapers Ltd 1995

Printed and bound in Great Britain by The Bath Press, Avon.

ISBN: 1-898-88515 X

Contents

For Heather

Editor's Preface

This is not a ghostwritten book. The words you are about to read are Stephen and Mae West's own. They originate in a series of long, detailed and sympathetic interviews with Stephen and Mae conducted by Gary Jones (Reporter Of The Year) and James Weatherup, one of *News Of The World's* most experienced writers.

We gave a lot of thought to how this material might best be presented in book form. Our purpose was to give a vivid and unfiltered insight into life at 25 Cromwell Street. That meant preserving Stephen's and Mae's own words, at whatever cost to smooth narrative and literary flourish. We have tried to place the reader in the position of someone sitting down with Stephen and Mae and gently asking the question: how did it happen?

There are inevitable difficulties in a book of this type, particularly with chronology. Some of the facts of the West case are still unclear. We do not know, for instance, when Catherine ('Rena'), Fred West's first wife, died. Other events in the 1970s and 1980s are equally difficult to place accurately.

We have therefore divided the book into three sections, reflecting the three most important phases of Stephen's and Mae's lives. The first and largest section deals with life at 25 Cromwell Street before the unearthing of the body of Heather,

Stephen's and Mae's elder sister, in a makeshift grave under some trees in the back garden.

Not all the memories are unhappy: there were seaside holidays, and all the rough and tumble of life in a large and noisy family. But the dark side was never far away—thieving expeditions, family upheavals, their mother's prostitution, their own period of physical and sexual abuse. Finally, there are the clues which, with hindsight, might have pointed more clearly to the reality behind their parents' behaviour.

The second section deals with the time after the discovery of Heather's body, leading up to Fred West's arrest, subsequent suicide, and the trial of Rosemary West. The final, shortest section deals with Rose West's trial, and the outcome.

In publishing this book, we have often been faced with the question of whether such an action can be justified. Why publish at all? Why not let the dead rest in peace, and allow the living to resume their lives?

The answer, it seemed to us, came in two parts. While many of the events at 25 Cromwell Street are horrific and extraordinary, others are more commonplace, if no more acceptable. The level of abuse suffered by the West children, particularly that suffered by the girls at the hands of their father, may be more common than many of us care to admit. There are anarchic and criminalised households in every community, where thieving and other lawbreaking are the norm. For as long as violence, abuse, and petty criminality are ignored or regarded as inevitable and untreatable, we will continue to discover more Fred Wests amongst us. Hannah Arendt, after witnessing the trial in Israel of the Nazi war criminal Adolf Eichmann, wrote of "the banality of evil". Her words resonate throughout this book, for this is a story of a suburban household of unremarkable appearance which nevertheless managed to embrace death on an unprecedented scale.

As well as banality, there is a continuity of evil which we ignore at our peril. The West family came into frequent contact with the police, criminal courts, social workers, schools, hospitals, employers, neighbours, victims who escaped. Yet the killing continued. The message is clear: anti-social behaviour left unchallenged or inadequately confronted leads to deeper problems, finally to deadly danger. If this book drives the point home, then that alone is justification for publication.

Secondly, it is clear to us that Stephen and Mae West are themselves two of the long list of victims of 25 Cromwell Street. They are alive, unlike their older sister and step-sister, and the ten other known victims of the Cromwell Street killing rampage. But they have suffered violence, terror, abuse and humiliation, and they deserve our sympathy.

Stephen and Mae intend to build new lives. They have well-developed plans for a better future. This book is part of their rehabilitation process.

-TG and PG
November 1995

The Two West Households

The First Household
Frederick West
Catherine ('Rena') West née Costello. First wife of Frederick West, married November 1962. Body found at Letterbox Field, Kempley, April 10, 1994.
Charmaine West. Older daughter of Rena but not Fred West. Body found May 4, 1994, under kitchen floor of Midland Road flat formerly occupied by Fred and Rose West.
Anne-Marie West. Daughter of Fred and Rena West. Sometimes referred to by Stephen and Mae as "Anna"

The Second Household
Frederick West
Rosemary ("Rose") West née Letts. Second wife of Frederick West, married January 1972.
Heather West. Oldest daughter of Fred and Rose West, born October 1970. Body found February 26, 1994 buried in back garden of 25 Cromwell Street.
Mae West. Daughter of Fred and Rose West. Born June 1972.
Stephen West. Oldest son of Fred and Rose West. Born August 1974.
Girl A. Daughter of Rose but not Fred West. Born 1977.
Girl B. Daughter of Fred and Rose West. Born 1978.
Boy C. Son of Fred and Rose West. Born 1979.
Girl D. Daughter of Rose but not Fred West. Born 1980.
Girl E. Daughter of Rose but not Fred West. Born 1981.
Boy F. Grandson of Fred and Rose West, son of Girl A.

Girl A, Girl B, Boy C, Girl D, Girl E and Boy F are, at the time of publication, all subject to a care order and, under English law, may not be named. In this book they are referred to as 'the kids' or 'the young kids'.

Book I
25 Cromwell St

Chapter 1
Fred and Rose

Mae...

Dad was born in Much Marcle in Herefordshire in 1943. He was the oldest, followed by his brothers John, David and Douglas and his sisters Kitty, Gwen and Daisy. All the kids were born in their front room at home. The family were tenant farmers and Walter, my granddad, leased their house in Much Marcle from the farmer who owned it. The West family lived there until 1992, but they had stopped farming by then and they lost the house. Dad was told that the farm would come to him; he was the eldest boy and should have taken it, but he turned it down. None of the brothers wanted it, but Doug took it on and lived there with his family and my granddad.

It was a really hard life when Dad was growing up. Their mother was a huge woman, really fat. She wore a massive leather belt and she was really strict. She was the boss in the family and eventually died of a heart attack, probably because of her size. They didn't have electricity or heating, just a little fire to boil the kettle.

They were a close family, and would fight for and protect each other. They went to church every Sunday, but they weren't particularly religious. It was a really basic life. If they wanted dinner they'd say 'see that pig over there? Go and kill it, we'll be eating it tonight'. I remember Dad telling us once how he had to kill the family pet pig for food. His Mum told him to do it. He told me he found it hard but he slit the pig's throat. He said it squealed and then ran around and dropped dead. After it was killed they hung it up in the kitchen and let the blood drip out of it for 12 hours.

Dad used to have to get up in the middle of the night to help the sheep when they were lambing. It was hard work—every day the kids had to get up really early and milk all the cows and see to the other animals before going to school. Dad said that when he was at school he used to stink of pigs' muck. He said he used to get picked on because he smelt and because he used to have to wear these huge hobnail boots which looked out of place. When we used to complain about our food Dad said all he got in his lunchbox was a raw turnip and parsnip.

Dad left school by the time he was fourteen, but he hardly ever went there anyway. He wasn't educated and could hardly even write. They didn't feel that they had to bother with school. They were farmers and were always going to be. After he left school, Dad used to stay at home and work around the farm, tending the stock and stuff.

Stephen...

Dad was well-liked within the family and, according to Uncle John, Dad was always easy-going and cheerful. But when he was sixteen he had a motorbike accident which completely changed him. Back in those days in 1959, you didn't have to wear a helmet on a motorbike and one day Dad missed a turning and lost control of his bike and smashed through a wall before hitting a tree. He was seriously injured and lay unconscious in a gully for eight hours until a passer-by spotted him and called an ambulance. He was taken to hospital where his heart stopped beating and a doctor pronounced him dead. To everyone's amazement, Dad came round on the mortuary slab and was resuscitated. He had a lot of injuries and had to have surgery. It was months before he could walk again.

Uncle John said that after the accident, Dad completely changed. He'd sit in the front room, staring at the wall and he wouldn't look at anyone, he wouldn't speak to anyone and if anyone spoke to him he'd bite their head off. He was so short-tempered that he couldn't control himself and he's been like that ever since.

Mae...

According to Dad, his dad Walter taught him it was a father's duty to "break in" his daughters. I don't know if it's true or not, but I do know that Dad claimed that when he was sixteen he tried it on with one of his sisters and he was charged by the police. Nothing came of the charge, so Dad said, but the family kicked Dad out, before he'd recovered from his accident.

No-one really knows where he went after that. I think he just scratched a living moving from job to job. He did come back to Much Marcle to try and make-up with his family, but no-one wanted to know him and he wasn't accepted back into the village.

Dad met Rena in 1962 when he was 19. She was from Glasgow and she was sent to an approved school there, a sort of borstal for girls. She'd got mixed up with this motorcycle gang called The Skulls and they were into drugs and everything, they were really rough. Rena met a girl in the school whose family was from Herefordshire. Rena was only in for a short time, and she was already pregnant with Charmaine. Charmaine's Dad was a student in Glasgow and he was really quite bright. He worked on the buses to earn a bit of extra money. It was only really a fling, nothing serious, and I don't think he knew Charmaine even existed until the police told him in 1994.

This other girl, Margaret, got out of the school first and went home to Ledbury. They kept writing to each other and when Rena got out of the school she followed Margaret to Ledbury where they both worked at the New Inn. That's where Rena met Dad. She and Dad started going out with each other and Margaret started seeing Uncle John.

Dad and Rena went out together for a couple of months and then they got married in November 1962. They both tried to get rid of the baby because it wasn't dad's, but Charmaine was born anyway in March 1963.

They went to Scotland to get away from all the village gossips and Dad drove an ice-cream van for a while as well as doing a milk round and delivering bread. They lived in the Gorbals in Glasgow, which is really rough. Their daughter Anne-Marie was born there in 1964, but the marriage was never that happy. They decided after a while to go back to Gloucester and they moved into a caravan site in Brockworth with the kids. Rena kept falling out with Dad, so she'd go to Scotland to stay with her family or friends and then come back and try to make it up with Dad.

Rena wanted the marriage to work, but Dad never really took it seriously and he was always seeing other women. He'd get home and tell Rena to get out to make room for the new woman he'd got with him. Dad used to beat her up and throw boiling hot tea over her if the dinner wasn't ready. But he drank a lot then.

Dad kicked Rena out for one of the victims, Annie McFall.

4

Annie came down from Scotland with them all as a nanny, but she was also Dad's girlfriend. She was really in love with him and Dad said to Stephen in prison that she was the only woman he ever loved, but he said that about Mum as well. I don't know why he killed her—I wasn't even born.

Dad met Mum in 1969 after he'd had another accident. A truck he'd been driving on a motorway construction site tipped over and he was sent to Cheltenham hospital for a check up. He wasn't badly hurt and they let him go home on the bus. That's when Dad met Mum.

When I went to see Mum at Pucklechurch Remand Centre before the trial, she told me all about it. Her name was Rose Letts then, and she was only 15. She was one of seven children: Pat, Joyce, Gwen, Andrew, Graham and Gordon. She lived at home in a three bedroomed house with her Dad, William, and her Mum, Daisy. They were quite a close family, but Mum's dad had been affected by the war a lot. He was weird, he used to buy sweets and the kids would think it was for them, then he'd sit and eat them all in front of them .

William had been in the Royal Navy and he used to bleach carpets and steam rooms, just as if he was on a ship. He used to have a scrub-out, shutting himself in a room and steaming it. The mother used to go mad about all the ruined carpets.

My grandmother is really religious, but my granddad wasn't particularly and they were always splitting up and then getting back together again. Really, Mum came from a broken home.

The kids were pushed to go to school, and they were expected to make a good marriage when they grew up—they were very respectable. Having said that, I think there was some

5

abuse in the family but Mum won't ever really talk about it, all she says is that her Dad hurt her once.

Mum told me she was once dropped off at her sister's house and the sister was told 'Don't tell Rosie where her Mum is'. Mum was only about 13 and I think that really hurt her.

This is how I remember Mum's story of how she and Dad got together:

"I was waiting at a bus stop when I noticed this man looking at me. I didn't take to him at all, he was dirty and had work clothes on and looked quite old.

I had just finished my day's work in a bread shop, it was dark and I was waiting to catch a bus home to my parent's house in Bishops Cleeve, a few miles out of Cheltenham.

This man started talking to me on the bus and just sat next to me without asking my permission. Within a few minutes he had asked me out. He was like a tramp, a real mess, and I said 'no'. I thought that was the end of that.

Soon after our first meeting I saw him again at the bus stop. He got on the bus with me and started asking me out to pubs which were near where I was working in the bread shop. One day a lady came into the shop and gave me present, saying a man had given it to her to give to me. It was something stupid, I can't remember what. Then Fred came in himself and shouted across the counter 'The Swallow—8pm'. That was my local pub and just a few minutes from where I lived. He'd obviously worked out that this was the best place for him to meet me.

Curiosity got the better of me and I went to the pub, thinking I'd give him back the present he had given me. I didn't have any feelings for him. We sat talking and drinking, that was all. He asked me out again and I agreed, so he took me to his caravan where he lived with his daughters Charmaine and Anne-Marie.

I asked Fred to meet my parents and they took an instant dislike to him when he came to our house. Mum said that he was ugly and had a bad attitude and was old with two kids whilst I was only fifteen. I wrote him a letter when my parents said they didn't like him. It said 'Go back to your wife and try and make a go of it'. But he didn't take any notice of the letter and turned up again at our door. I began to fall in love with him; he was so persistent and I was flattered by his determination to be with me. I started to see him in secret.

Often when I went to the caravan Fred would have women there who were supposed to be looking after Charmaine and Anne-Marie. But most of them were sleeping with Fred. A lot of them were girls from my school. I chucked them all out, together with the trunk of womens' underwear he had at the back of the caravan.

A month after my sixteenth birthday, I discovered I was pregnant with Heather. I told my parents and I got a beating that I'll never forget. Dad wanted me to have an abortion. My parents made my life a misery.

Next, my parents arranged for me to be put in a home for a time to make sure that Fred and I were separated. Whilst I was there I heard that Dad had beaten up Mum and they had split up. Their marriage was always rocky.

I went through a very rough period. I stayed with my mother for a while, then I was put back in a home, but conned my way out by pretending to have seen the error of my ways. I told my parents that I didn't want to see Fred again and that I would get rid of the baby. I deliberately locked myself away in my room and pretended that I was ashamed of myself for becoming pregnant. I wouldn't look my parents in the face.

Mum and Dad took out a court injunction to keep Fred away from me. They got the court's backing because he had under age sex with me. But he broke the order in any case.

Without discussing it with me, my father booked me into an abortion clinic. I decided I had to meet Fred and tell him what was happening. I made an excuse that I needed to go into town to buy some things for the hospital and they believed me and gave me some money. Fred was working at a tyre fitters and I met up with him. We hatched this plan where, instead of getting into the ambulance that my parents had arranged, I would run round the corner and meet him in his car. That was our plan, but it didn't go like that. Dad came up to my room later that day and gave me an ultimatum. He said: 'You can get rid of the baby, stay at home with your Mum and Dad, have no boyfriends, pay your own way, and everything will be all right, or you can leave now with this Fred West bloke and you will never see your Mum or Dad again. And if I see you in the street, I'll knife you'.

Dad had made these threats before and had once said he would burn down Fred's caravan with us both in it if he caught us together there. Staying at home didn't sound much fun, so I packed two carrier bags, kissed Dad goodbye and then went to the kitchen and tried to cuddle Mum. But she was furious and said to me: 'What do you think you're doing?' My brothers Gordon and Graham waved me off; we were quite close.

Fred had rented a flat in Cheltenham but it was a real pit. We were all in this little room together; me, Fred, and his kids Anne-Marie and Charmaine. It was impossible to live there because it was so small. There was just a tiny sink in the corner. It was hopeless. Fred suggested we move to Gloucester because Cheltenham folk didn't take kindly to unmarried families.

We moved to Midland Road in 1970, just outside the town centre, where there were a lot of Jamaicans living. That was my first experience of coloured people. My parents came to visit us there and tried to make up with us. Midland Road was a ground floor flat with a garden in the back where the children could play.

Heather was born and Fred started doing repair work for the man we rented the flat from. Then Fred went to prison for car crimes. I was only 18, and I was pregnant again, with you (ie Mae: ed). I had a 12-month-old baby, Heather, and I had Charmaine and Anne-Marie to look after, all in a one-bedroom flat. I made a good friend with the lady upstairs, but I felt very alone, especially at night, and money was really tight.

Fred was released from prison and our landlord offered us the chance to buy 25 Cromwell Street, which we bought for £7,000. Because I was pregnant again, I thought we'd better get married to make things legal.

We married in January 1972. Even the marriage was rushed. Fred was fixing an old car half an hour before we were due at the Registry Office. I had to beg him to take off his overalls.

His brother John witnessed the marriage, and another friend of Fred's who had so many aliases he had to scribble out the first name he wrote on the certificate. On the way back, Fred found some money in the park which covered the cost of the marriage licence. I remember he was over the moon.

We had no honeymoon. We just went to the Wellington pub and he bought one drink. He asked me what I wanted, and I said a lager and lime. He said 'You have a bloody Coke and like it.'

Mae was born in June. We didn't move into Cromwell Street until September because the place was in such a mess. It wasn't derelict, but it was run down."

Mae ...

Mum doesn't like speaking about those days. She says that everything now has painful memories for her. Charmaine was killed at Midland Road and her body was found under the kitchen floor. But that's the bit that's so confusing. Mum says this woman came to collect Charmaine, and she thought it was Rena. It could have been anyone, really. Somehow Dad got this woman to get Charmaine away from the house. I can't understand how Charmaine went, and then somehow was buried under the kitchen, when Mum was staying in that flat? But it was a long time ago, so it must be difficult for Mum to remember.

Although Mum knew about Rena, she says that she thought that Rena had gone back to Scotland. When she married Dad he put 'bachelor' on the marriage certificate and because Mum was so young, I don't think she ever really asked whether they were divorced. She was happy to take on the two kids; she says she felt sorry for them and made sure they were well looked after, clothed and fed. Dad had more kids up in Scotland. When we were young he said he had 42 . He claimed he'd killed one by backing his ice-cream van over it, but no-one has ever found any evidence of it. The only other kid of his that Mum looked after is his son Steve McAvoy who's in his thirties now. Dad brought him down to Gloucester once when he was about eight years old. We were only babies then. Mum said that he was still in nappies and that she toilet trained him and stuff and then sent him home.

I've never kept in touch with my grandmother. Once Mum and Dad started having half-caste children, our grandmother asked Mum not to come around any more. I know Mum tried writing to her, but the letters went unanswered. Mum had almost no contact at all with her mum, which I know she regretted.

After a while though, Dad's family began talking to him again and we used to visit them as kids. They were still leading a really basic life. I noticed that they used to hang tea-bags up to dry so that they could recycle them. We used to play with Uncle Doug's kids, our cousins, but other than that it was only really Uncle John who came to see us at Cromwell Street. He used to work as a bin man and bring us toys from the tip because we didn't have any.

Mum's parents split up, though not because of Dad, and for a while Mum's dad and my dad got on quite well. They even ran a cafe together, but it didn't work out.

I think Mum did really love Dad. She had to, to go through so much to marry him. I have read some of the letters they wrote to each other and they're terribly romantic. Dad had a tattoo on his arm; it was a love heart with 'Rena' and 'Fred' written on it, but he scratched 'Rose' over the top of Rena's name.

Chapter 2
25 Cromwell St

Frederick West's criminal record dated back to 1961 when, aged 18, he was fined £4 at Ledbury Magistrates' Court on two counts of theft. He was caught nine times between 1961 and 1980 for either theft or handling stolen goods. He was sent to prison for six months in December 1970 for a series of motoring offences and theft. Stephen, who was forced to accompany his father on stealing sprees says: "He stole anything he could get his hands on. He was an incredible thieving machine." Mae, from the age of seven, also accompanied her father on these trips .

Mae...

He would see a pile of bricks or cement in the road and go back that night when it was dark and load them into his van. Practically the whole of our house extension was made from stolen goods, right down to the wooden support beams which held the roof up. He was quite open about it; he never liked to pay for anything.

When he did repair jobs in peoples' houses, he'd leave a latch open on a window and later that night he'd steal objects he had liked the look of. Our house was full of ornaments which he'd claim he had been given by a satisfied customer. At one time we had seven video recorders, the same number of televisions, and loads of radio cassette players in the house.

He loved hoarding and would buy dodgy gear from a bloke he knew. At least 99% of the contents of the house were stolen, including the lino on the floor.

Another scheme he had was to order too much building materials for jobs and when he had finished, he would take the surplus home for his own use. Mum and Dad had a beautiful pine bar upstairs in Mum's room, and all the wood had been pinched. He refused to spend his money on anything. He moaned if he had to spend 50 pence.

Stephen ...

When we outgrew our bikes, Dad took me out to steal new ones. He took me to this park, never for fun, but just to nick bikes. He would walk 100 yards in front of me and break the bike lock very quickly without anyone seeing what he was doing. I'd have to follow behind and ride the bike to the van where we'd meet up. We'd get them for the whole family. To be honest I never thought we were doing anything wrong, it was normal family life for us.

Dad would steal anything, whether it was locked up or not. He'd drive out to building sites at midnight and pinch things for the extension he was building. He never paid for anything if he could steal it. The entire roof was stolen, in fact I can't remember him ever paying for anything from a shop.

He endlessly nicked building material from his boss Derek. If Dad got his hands on some blue paint the whole house would be done up with it. It was the same with a cheap bit of carpet. The whole hallway was done up with Derek's stuff and when he came round we had to put up sheets to hide everything Dad had pinched. Dad wouldn't even pay for bus or train tickets. Funnily enough, it wasn't really the money that made him do it, he gave his complete wage packet to Mum. He wouldn't spend a penny on himself, it was a compulsion, just like a magpie which steals anything that's shiny and available. He didn't need the stuff he stole, most of it was useless. For example, he stole one of those mirrors used by drivers so they can see round a blind bend in the road, and put it up on his bedroom ceiling—presumably to watch himself having sex.

Dad even stole from his workmates, and I think they guessed that was the case, but they couldn't prove it. He often took ladders and tools from his neighbours.

Even when he was on remand in Birmingham in early 1993, Dad would rig phone boxes so that he could speak to Mum for hours without spending a penny. He walked round Birmingham for hours at a time. God knows what he was doing. He told us he hit his head on a sign while walking round and sued the AA for £250. He said he had suffered blackouts and seizures in his arms.

At home, Dad would never sit still, he was hyperactive. He'd get in from work and take a shower and then take his time to dry. He'd be naked and then he'd put his underpants on and sit down and watch TV.

He'd always grope Mum in front of us. She only minded if he had dirty hands. It was just their way. They saw it as a joke, but we didn't. You've never seen a table cleared so quick. It would be a case of 'Dad's groping mum, we're off.'
Mae...

Dad would never wear clothes that Mum bought for him. He liked to wear clothes he found while out working. Mum bought him jeans and he used one pair as a draught excluder for seven years before finally getting round to wearing them. That's how much he took care of his clothes and appearance.

He even wore dead men's clothes, like Mum's Dad's shoes, even though they were too small for him. I remember him saying, when he was trying them on, 'Look, Rose, they're still warm'.

He didn't have a particularly kind word to say about Mum's Mum either. Once, he was fixing the curtains in our bedroom and he stood on a chair which had been a present from our grandmother. It was a very old one and when he stood too far back it fell forward, hitting him in the stomach. He wasn't breathing and Heather stayed with him while I ran downstairs to get help. I couldn't get my breath to tell Mum he was hurt, but she guessed there was a problem and ran upstairs just as he was getting his breath back. He told her 'Your Mum's trying to kill me. She always hated me'.

His eating habits were also strange; he used to eat really weird things if he got home early from work. He'd cut a huge end off a loaf of bread and put big slabs of cheese on the top. He'd eat an onion like it was an apple. He'd also spread a thick lump of lard from the chip pan onto a piece of bread and eat the thick, really blubbery, part of the meat. It was awful what he'd eat. Mum is really fussy about what she cooks, and if she didn't like the look of something she'd just chuck it in the bin. Dad would shout 'No, Rose, that's perfect', then he'd grab the bin and start eating out of it, and he'd offer it to us kids.

Dad was always coming home with odd sweets and he'd give them to Stephen. After Stephen had eaten them Dad would say 'I found that in some dogs muck' and Stephen would rush off and throw up.

He used to call the toilet his conference room. He'd call us in while he was on the toilet and we'd have to sit on the edge of the bath and talk to him. He was just totally open about things.

One time he accused me of trying to poison him. I was making him something to eat and I put a knife from the scramble egg mix back into the butter. He was convinced for some reason this was going to kill him and he went absolutely berserk. He said 'Don't bother cooking anything for me any more'.

The restrictions on my life really used to get me down. Silly things, like him not allowing me, Heather and Stephen to even be together. He'd say there was something wrong with us if we were laughing and playing together. He didn't like us talking to Mum, especially me. I wasn't allowed to talk to her alone for some reason.

He was obsessive about other things as well. He was always going out to the van during the night to clean it and top up the oil and water.

He talked endlessly about animals and their breeding habits. I think it went back to his childhood when he was brought up on a farm and got some funny sexual ideas about them.

He claimed to have had sex with a sheep. He was talking about doing it and his description was very detailed. He said there was an art to it and you needed long wellies. 'You can put their back feet inside the wellies with yours, then they can't move,' that's what he told us anyway.

He was always working on the house. He was planning to decorate the basement as rooms and a bedroom for him and Mum and he loved standing out in the front of Cromwell Street so he could talk to passers-by. He could talk the hind legs off a donkey and often ended up taking complete strangers round the house. It didn't matter to him what sort of person they were, whether they were drunks or down and outs. He even

17

showed them our bedrooms. He liked people to say what a nice home he had. He would give tramps in the street sugar and tea bags. In our road we had a lot of people who had been released from a mental hospital, and they were shown round as well. Mum didn't like them mixing with us children. Once he sold me to one of them for £1. He was serious. The chap came back for me, and Mum had to tell him to get lost. Dad also tried to get couples into our house and asked them if they wanted to watch some of his dirty videos.

Dad was always going on at Mum about sleeping with other men. It started two days after they got married. He nagged and nagged her to do it, so eventually she gave in. I remember when I was about 13 or 14 she started working as a prostitute. I think her attitude was that if she had to sleep with other men, she might as well get money for the house and for us, and it kept it purely professional.

She and Dad placed an advert in a sex magazine and in it she called herself Mandy. I often answered the phone when clients called. It was a bit confusing at first because they were all asking for Mandy, but Mum warned me that they would be calling. She said that I should take their name and numbers and tell them that Mandy would call them back. She told me to put the phone down if they started talking dirty. She didn't explain why they were calling, but we weren't thick and we soon worked it out. The men on the phone would rattle on about the things that they wanted and ask how much Mandy charged.

In the beginning there were lots of men coming, maybe ten a week, I'm not sure. They were all different ages and colours. Mum wouldn't let us answer the door but I could see some looked very nervous. I remember one of them had a hole in his hand, one a peg leg and another had a glass eye. They were loners really. The front doors were kept locked and there were two doorbells, one for the family and one for 'Mandy', which would ring directly at Mum's flat.

Mum occupied the top two floors of the house. There were two bedrooms on the top floor, and a lounge, a kitchen and a bathroom on the next floor down. Dad did it up really well— it was the smartest part of the house. We weren't allowed in it. Dad said we would wreck it.

Mum's lounge used to be Shirley Robinson's room. It had a bar in one corner in a Jamaican style and a black magic sign on the top, several optics and drinks on a shelf, all done in a dark oak. Dad made it over several months until he got the parts for it. My ex-boyfriend Rob made and painted the black magic sign with gold palm trees on it. Stephen got hold of other bits and pieces, like the optics, from working at a wine warehouse. There was a picture covering a whole wall of some sandy beach, a paradise type of place, which I remember was quite expensive. It gave a tropical theme for the bar. In the room there was a two-seater chair, a television, video and stereo unit and a dark oak wall unit which was seven feet tall, on which were china objects Mum had either been given over the years, or which Dad had stolen. There are a lot of homes where Dad worked which will have missed favourite ornaments at one time or another.

Mum put everything on display and knew her 'presents' from Dad had not been bought specially for her from a high street store. I never liked the decoration of the house, but it suited Mum and Dad. There were tiger skins on the floor and a chandelier-type light, making it look like a brothel.

One of the bedrooms had a four-poster bed, which Dad made

19

on a lathe. The rest of the stuff he put together over several nights during the week. The four of us stood holding the posts while he fitted it together, making sure it would stand the strain. The bed looked nice until you saw the word 'cunt' which Dad had cut out at work in welded metal and fixed on the front pelmet of the bed. There were four bulls, one on top of each post of the bed. On the side he had stuck a bull and a cow together as though they were having sex. They were farm-yard toys. This is where Mum and Dad mostly slept together.

The other bedroom had a king-size bed with a lace canopy. Mum moved into the king size bedroom if Dad was hogging the bed or if people were staying overnight when she was prostituting.

The room looked fairly normal apart from the microphones hidden in speakers, which had been placed in the black beams that Dad had put up in the ceiling. Dad also built a micro-phone into the bed so he could listen to Mum when she had clients.

There was a concave mirror on the ceiling and several pine units with marble tops. On the wall there were two pictures of cows that fascinated Dad. He wanted me to paint some bulls to go in the middle of them. You couldn't get away from sex. Every door in Mum's part of the house had a picture of a half-naked or naked woman on the back. The house was pretty shabby before Mum started working as a prostitute, but once she started earning money, they started spending money around the house. Dad didn't care about our part, it was all brown paint and cheap carpets which he'd change every six months because they'd get in such a mess.

As we got older, Mum started to confide in me and she told me that one of her clients liked her to sit in a clear mac and

talk to him, nothing else. We had to search all over Gloucester to find her a clear mac to wear. She used to put on her
underwear and stuff upstairs and wear her dressing gown over
it so we couldn't see. Sometimes I used to get a glimpse of
them leaving but Mum would slam the door if we were standing near the hallway. I never saw her take money but some of
the men used to stay the night so that must have cost a bit.

I tried to stay out of their way but I remember once when I
opened my bedroom door as one client was passing and Mum
pushed me back in, but not before he had the chance to ask if
'that one was available'. I was only about thirteen. Mum
kicked this guy straight out. When Dad found out he was really keen and said 'that's a good idea'.

Mum had a red and black book in which she would keep all
their statistics—penis size, performance and all the names.
Stephen picked the lock on their bedroom door once and we
read it. There were about 70 names. Mum and Dad also had
an album of about 25 polaroid pictures of men's erect private
parts which were usually kept locked in a briefcase.

Mum started to get her flat together upstairs and she spent a
lot of money on it. There was one man in particular who used
to come to our house all the time, he was one of the freebies.
He was one of Dad's old friends, and he used to come around
whenever it suited him, usually Sunday lunch time. Mum
didn't even like him—she said it made her sick going to bed
with him—but Dad made her do it. He used to grind her down,
night after night, telling her she was a bad wife if she didn't
do things for her husband.

Every Sunday Mum cooked dinner and he always came
round when she was preparing it. We knew when the doorbell
went on a Sunday what was going to happen next. It used to

really piss us off because it would be a really nice dinner, and when Mum went upstairs Dad would finish cooking it, and he always ruined it. There would be lumps in the gravy that were like potatoes underneath, but they were cornflour balls when you cut into them. Once I was old enough I'd take over the cooking instead, though I had to physically fight him to do it.

Dad couldn't have cared less about cooking dinner because he was more interested in what Mum was doing. He'd get a speaker from the shelf which was connected to a long extension lead. He had rigged up the speaker to a microphone which he'd connected up to the headboard in mum's bed. It was like a baby intercom but more sophisticated. He would sit on the sofa with the speaker next to his ear, just listening. No-one was allowed to speak to him while Mum was with a client. We used to keep turning up the television to drown out the groaning noises from upstairs. We just wanted to watch Tom and Jerry.

There were speakers wired throughout the house—every room had one—so Dad could keep tabs on us. They had a receiver up in the bedroom as well so he could hear up there what was going on in the rest of the house. He had this white box which could pick up all the rooms at once. It had numbers on it, but we never touched it. It would have been more than our lives were worth.

We occasionally met some of the men who went with mum. They seemed OK, and weren't perverts. They just sat with us, playing, before Mum was ready to see them. While she was working I would look after the younger children. It would only be for an hour at a time and usually two or three times during the day when she disappeared upstairs. She would tell me to look after them and get them dressed. When the door-bell went we knew there was someone coming, so we would be quiet. She would go to the front door and lock the upstairs door to the flat behind her. She told me if I ever needed her urgently to knock loudly and she would come down. She did come down after about half an hour to check on us and then she would go back up. Once she had established a few regulars, they knew me and they were alright. She didn't have to go so often, and they'd have set times when they came round. We got used to her going upstairs for only a couple of hours a day after that.

Often when Mum was busy with a client, Dad would pop his head round the corner after coming in from work and say 'where's your mother?' If we said upstairs, he knew what we meant and would start unwinding the speakers and listening to Mum having sex. He sometimes put his ear to the doorway to hear what was going on.

Stephen...

She made a note of what she charged and it seemed as if she gave them marks out of ten. It was written very neatly in rows, like accounts. She also used to order men from the book. If she fancied a coloured bloke who was well endowed she would look it up and ring them instead. You could hear her call and count the minutes until there was a ring at the door. There was a red album and also a money box with a key attached by a piece of string. When I opened it, I found a bundle of pictures of Dad lying naked on the bed and Mum naked with other men. I was shocked at seeing these pictures, but I knew that sort of stuff was going on and I knew what Mum and Dad were like. The polaroid pictures showed close-ups of Mum having sex with a close friend. I think Dad took the pictures; they must have been posed to have taken them so close. Some topless pictures of Mum were in a wooden glass-fronted cabinet. They were sort of modelling ones. Mum's friend in the pictures is very well endowed. Dad always mentioned that he was the best.

If a client stayed overnight Dad would sleep on the settee downstairs listening on the intercom to what was going on. There was a lot of talking and screaming usually and all the sessions were secretly filmed. They used to have a red light in one of the rooms—not to say that she was open for business; she didn't have people off the street—but to add to the atmosphere. Mum and Dad used to watch their home-made blue movies for their own entertainment and they didn't show them to anyone else. I looked at one once, it was vile. Mum was on the kitchen table sitting on some cushions with her legs apart and she was using her vibrator. Then she got some tea towels put them on the table and starting urinating everywhere. It was revolting. She was enjoying it, playing with herself and obviously Dad was filming it. They also took videos of Mum with other men in the back of the van when she was tied up. I watched one when I was 17 after I found it upstairs. Dad tied up mum, whipped her and then had sex with her. I felt totally repulsed, turned it off and walked away. When their friends called around, they would all go out in the van together. Dad even put a little gas fire and carpet in the back of the van because it got so cold. Then they would take a flask of tea and his usual bag of sex aids. I think Dad used to drive along when Mum was having sex in the back and he'd film it on a tripod that he had bolted to the back. This would happen throughout the year. Sometimes they would go out at ten at night and we would look after ourselves. It was usually on a Saturday night. They didn't say where they were going and we didn't ask any questions. We were always told to make things safe, like turn the fires down, make sure that the TV and video were switched off and the doors were locked.

We could always hear them come in. They weren't quiet coming in, they weren't quiet at doing anything. As far as they were concerned, no-one else lived in the world apart from them. They would come in laughing and joking and go up-stairs; Mum's friend used to stay the night. Dad would go to work about eight in the morning; he never seemed tired but now and then he would come home and fall asleep. Mum used to sleep during the day.

Mae...

In the end I think she whittled it down to four regulars. The sessions usually lasted an hour or two hours. I didn't mind the hourly ones which I think cost about £15. But when you are kids time seemed to drag and when you've had your Mum around you, you wanted her back. We could only disturb her if there was an emergency and she thought we were old enough to look after ourselves. That usually meant it was mainly my job to look after our four younger brothers and sisters. So I had to keep the kids entertained, but if Mum was upstairs a long time they got whingey; they wanted their Mum.

Stephen...

Mum used to have her window open when she was working and you could hear her from the street. It was embarrassing to go to the shop. When we were a bit younger we used to sit at night and talk about it between us. We would ask whether Mum was sleeping with these blokes or just talking to them because we were still fairly innocent kids and we weren't sure what was happening. I mean you knew, but you didn't like to admit it. Being the eldest Heather would say 'they're doing it alright, why do you think your sister is half-caste?'

When she had finished she always used to be a lot more relaxed, happier and polite. I remember when Dad was listening to it on the speaker he would just sit there like he was listening to the radio or watching telly. He wouldn't want to speak to anyone. In the summer holidays once, I got the job of painting the fireplace while Dad decorated elsewhere. We had the radio on but when the doorbell would go Dad would turn it off and say 'work quietly your Mum is upstairs'. To us kids it was nothing, it happened all the time, we would hear all the loud noises up and down the stairs and just carry on with whatever we were doing.

Mae...

They started improving the house in 1986 for what Dad called 'Mum's privacy'. Mum says she earned enough money as a prostitute to complete the work upstairs. They must have spent thousands on all the improvements.

I never felt comfortable in Cromwell Street. It was home, but never really a home where you felt warm and safe. To Dad, 25 Cromwell Street was the most precious thing in his life.

Chapter 3
Childhood

Some of the victims of 25 Cromwell Street were lodgers who stayed in the house only a matter of weeks. Shirley Robinson, the last known victim before Heather, disappeared in 1979 when Stephen and Mae were five and seven years old respectively. They have no specific memories of Lucy Partington (1973), Lynda Gough (1973), Carol Ann Cooper (1973), Shirley Hubbard (1974), Therese Siegenthaler (1974) or Juanita Mott (1975), all of whom disappeared when they were infants. Nor do they recall Alison Chambers (1979), who disappeared when Mae was seven years old, and Stephen was five.

Mae...

Dad's attitude was that us kids were just there, we weren't meant to stop him from doing anything in his life. He didn't plan us and I don't think he really wanted us. He never knew where we were or how many he had. We were just there. I think we just made a good cover for him.

Our oldest half-sister Anne-Marie left home when she was sixteen. I was only about seven or eight at the time and I don't remember much, but she was always in trouble with the police and she was head of this gang. They were into drinking and the police kept coming round saying that Anna had done something.

She and Mum didn't get on well. They were more like sisters because of the small age gap and Anna wouldn't do as she was told; she used to say 'You're not my mum'. Anna thought that Rena would have made a better mum and so when she turned sixteen she left home. She disappeared for years and no-one knew where she was, then she came back with her boyfriend Chris and said she was going to marry him. That was about five or six years after she left.

My memories of growing up are just of me, Heather and Stephen and the five younger kids in the house.

Stephen ...

We always knew we were different. There was no such thing as normal. I remember my sister vacuuming at the age of eight. It was the way we were and what was expected of us, the children. Mum and Dad would say 'If you are going to live here...' and then they would give us a job to do. And another famous one was 'If you don't like it—you know where the door is'. That was their answer to everything.

I was only about seven years old when I was taught how to do the washing. Mum would show us how to separate the different colours so they didn't run, scrub the collars of the shirts first, and then how to set the machine. At the same age we would be doing the ironing. Sometimes we came very close to hurting ourselves badly, but the main thing was not making any mistakes. You made sure you were very careful. Sometimes you would only have to do your own clothes, but if you had been bad Mum would give you everyone's to do. The whole family! It took ages.

Our parents taught us how to fend for ourselves at a very

early age, though only because that meant they could go out knowing that we would be all right. We used to babysit when I was young and we would change the babies' nappies and feed them. By then I was pretty independent and could set the video. At the age of nine I could put on a three point plug. Dad taught me that. I set up a big six foot square circuit board in my bedroom and wired it all up before plugging it into the mains. It was brilliant fun. Other kids wouldn't have been allowed to do that because it would have been considered too dangerous, but Dad let me do anything I wanted. He didn't take too much notice because he was at work so much.

I find children spend a lot more time in their bedroom if they don't feel comfortable with their parents. That was the position with me. I did everything in my bedroom just to keep away from the madness of my Mum and Dad. My bedroom was everything I stood for, it was my hideaway where for a few hours I was safe from everything that was happening around me.

But you could never hide away for long as there was always something to do around the house. I had the living room to clean up, vacuum and dust. One of us would do the kitchen, the washing-up and wash the kitchen floor. And the other one would scrub the bathroom floor and clean the whole bathroom. We had to clean the inside of the toilets, putting our whole arm in and really scrubbing. We didn't have a rota but we knew what we had to do. Mae, Heather and I had to decide how to split up the work. We did all this from as far back as I can remember. Mum would show us how to do jobs properly and we would stand watching her every move, like hawks watching rabbits. If we did it wrong, she would give us a clout and we wouldn't do it wrong again. She wouldn't let you hurt yourself, but she made sure you knew exactly how to do it right. We wouldn't dare do it wrong. There was also the washing: how to set the machine and how much powder to put in. As young children we thought it was all a bit much for us, but we learnt and we learnt quickly. I've never been afraid of hard work because of our childhood. If you weren't doing something in our household, you were lazy and useless.

Saturdays and Sundays weren't a lot different from the rest of the week. We may not have had to go to school but we had more housework to do. We all had to clean our rooms which would take a couple of hours if we did it properly. Sunday lunch would be at about 2pm when we'd just finished our washing. After tea we polished our shoes for school, showered and went to bed. You had to stay up until you had done all these jobs. There were odd times when I didn't finish or it wasn't done properly and Mum would make me do it all again. We seemed to be kept busy all the time.

I knew my life wasn't like that of my mates. When I was eleven I was given the cellar room. I had no fancy wallpaper or fancy fittings. It was an empty room with bare plaster board on the walls. There weren't even any light shades. Dad just said: 'That's yours now, son, get on with it'.

First I started off saving from paper rounds for materials. I used to make furniture by sketching the units I saw at B & Q. I would get the leaflet on the sizes and everything and then buy wood and do it myself. I would learn how to do the joints from drawings in DIY books. It took months and months to do all the work. Then I saved up for wallpaper and I sorted out the ceiling and put coving up. By the time I had finished I had a really nice room.

I enjoyed the work and the sense of achievement it gave me, and also it got me away from the rest of the household. My sisters would get me to do work in their rooms too. They would pay me in sweets or whatever. I enjoyed the freedom of doing it. I thought I was privileged to do all this. I liked the idea of everyone being envious of me at school because I could do my own room up. I don't know if they were, I doubt it very much, but I thought I was really grown up and it made me proud of myself. I used to take photos of what I had done and show them to mates at school. A lot of them thought I was lying.

I have still got, to this day, an old 1978 wiring book which I had memorised. I read this book so many times before I went to bed, I knew everything. I knew the electrics had to be off first and that you had to double check everything before you put it back on. I was always in B & Q, to me it was like going into a sweet shop. I knew where you could find everything. It wasn't weird for me at all. I suppose they must have thought I was buying for my dad. If I wanted help I tried to catch Dad in a good mood and ask him. I had a problem with a two-way switch once because I had no books on it. Luckily Dad was trying to be helpful at the time and he told me what I needed and how to do it. I made sure I remembered everything he said and then went away and did it. That was the bit I liked about growing up. I know it's not much, but to me it was important.

As kids we quickly learnt that if you wanted something you had to do it yourself. We would be given bus money but we were reluctant to give anything away and used to walk to school. The three of us, Mae and Heather and I would do the four miles there, four miles back. I used to save my bus money and my paper round wage to buy a roll of wallpaper or wood. Everyone else my age was buying Airfix models or whatever. I was never interested in any of that stuff. I never had toys in my room, never. I couldn't be bothered with toy cars or making models.

Mum seemed to think her role was to keep control of everything and make sure we didn't step out of line. I'm surprised I didn't join the Army. It would have been the perfect career for me.

Mum was the boss when Dad wasn't around and she never let us forget the fact. She would lose her temper all the time. Can you imagine anything more ridiculous than her going crazy over where she had put the dishcloth? She would stand in the middle of the kitchen shouting 'Dishcloth, dishcloth, dishcloth, dishcloth'. When anything went missing she would shout at the top of her voice and we would come running. The mission was to find whatever she was looking for, on the double, at all costs. To even have thoughts of failure would be a big mistake. We were petrified. Anyway, we would look everywhere for this dishcloth. We were like bees buzzing around all over the place trying to find the thing. She was frantic, totally out of control. What was so ridiculous was that the dishcloth was more often than not hanging over her shoulder where she had left it. We'd be too scared to tell her. We'd rush around like crazy until she found where it was, and then without saying anything she'd go back to what she was doing before. It was the same with spoons. If she couldn't find a little spoon she'd go ballistic. You could hear her from up the street, she was so loud. If you found the spoon and handed it to her she'd rip it from your hand. None of us would look at her while she was behaving like this, because if we did she'd say

'What are you looking at?' These explosions were on a daily basis. You had to be there to believe them.

Mae...

We knew our life was different, but we weren't envious of others. This was our lot and we were going to do the best we could. The saying 'What you never have you never miss' was spot on as far we were concerned.

For Christmas and birthdays we would only get one present. Mum and Dad had no money so if we got nothing, we knew the reason why. All the money they had was spent doing up the house. That was something we accepted, it wasn't anything to do with us in any case.

Entertainment was going to the Kings Walk fountains in Gloucester where we would fish around in the water for two pence pieces people had thrown in for good luck. Mum took us to the fountains once. We were in our swimming costumes and all of us kids jumped in and swam round. Then we got out, towelled ourselves off and got dressed. The shoppers stopped and looked at us but we didn't care what anyone thought.

We were picked on at school because we looked so poor; the way we were dressed. We couldn't have deodorant until we were sixteen. It wasn't as if Mum was spending any money on herself. She washed her hair in vinegar and we used washing-up liquid. We'd get a grant for the uniform because we had so little money. It was always Co-op starched shirts and every item of clothing was three sizes too big like a clown's suit. Mum told us 'You'll grow into them'."

Stephen...

We wore really old fashioned clothes. Mum bought my jeans from Oxfam, big flared things. We were called the Walton's because we wore dungarees. They were cut off in the summer. We had one set of school clothes and one set of play clothes and that was our wardrobe. If I ruined anything it would be replaced at Oxfam. I had two pairs of trousers and a couple of shirts. That was the sum total. The girls didn't have any more clothes than I did. My four younger brothers and sisters had loads of clothes as they were growing up.

Mae...

Mum got milder as we got older and the younger kids were spoilt compared to us. I never had anything pretty to wear. All our toys came from Uncle John who did a dustbin round. He used to bring us things he'd saved from the tip. I even had to wear boys' shoes because they were harder wearing. I showed Dad my new school shoes once and he just threw them against the wall. He said it was bad luck to put new shoes on the table. We'd even have short back and sides as Mum couldn't handle combing long hair.

We had free school dinners and felt really poor when our classmates found out. They were always taking the mickey out of us. I lost my bus pass in the first week of school once. It cost about £15 and we couldn't pay for another one, so I had to go to school on the back of Dad's moped. Mum was cross and I felt really upset. It was terrible because Dad made me wear this white helmet. I was so embarrassed. When I got my next bus pass Mum tied it to my satchel with elastic. I used to get on the bus, pull it out and then it would ping back and hit me. Mum did that with our gloves as well so we wouldn't lose them. All my friends used to take the mickey out of me.

They were the only parents who wanted us to stay home

from school. I got a belting for going to school once, when they wanted me to help lay the basement floor. Stephen stayed off school but I didn't want to. Dad never went to school events, like sports day. We used to beg him to go. They didn't go to anything.

Stephen...

We'd keep to ourselves at school and I suppose Mae and I were soft and like school creeps. Mum and Dad weren't keen on us having an education, let alone teaching us themselves. There was no reading or writing at home or help with our homework.

I was about twelve when I had to help lay the floor. They used to encourage me not to go to school. 'If you don't want to go—don't go,' I was told. They never went to parents' evenings. Mum would read my school reports and if one was bad she gave me a slapping and if they were good she would say nothing and put them away. It was very disheartening. We could never tell Mum what we'd done at school. I was quite keen on the once-a-year sports day and did quite well at running. If you started talking to Dad about it he'd tell you to shut up. He had no interest whatsoever in what we achieved, he only looked for failure.

I was aware of what Mum was like from an early age. At the infants school we put on a school play every Friday morning and all the mums watched us perform, except mine. I can't remember a time when she ever showed any interest in what I was doing. I often begged her 'Please, Mum, come and see me' and very occasionally she said 'OK, then' but she never came. The teachers asked why Mum never turned up and I would tell them she was too busy looking after my brothers and sisters.

Mae...

I did really well at school but Dad couldn't have cared less. Dad never once looked at anything I did at school. He was never interested and if I shoved some work I was proud of under his face he'd chuck it out the way.

There was nothing I could do to please him, unless it was something for him. He wanted me to paint him a bull to go with his cow picture upstairs in his bedroom, but I only got half way through it. There was no enjoyment doing anything for him. I realise now how very selfish he was. He never remembered us growing up, our birthdays, or even our names. He couldn't even remember how many children he had. If someone asked him, he would say 'six or seven'. He never called us by our names, it was always 'Anna, er Heather, er Mae, oh whoever you are, make me a cup of tea'. He only recognised Stephen because he was his boy. He'd call him nicknames like Dizzy Homo, or Daisy or Delilah, because he knew it annoyed him.

He even called Mum names and never used Rose or Mum. His favourite was 'old cow'. It was not said nastily, but simply as if it was her real name. He'd also call her 'dragon' and would say 'come here dragon and make me a cup of tea' or 'where's my tea, dragon?'.

What really annoyed us was when strangers came round, Dad would tear strips off us in front of them. He'd say 'There's my daughter, I think she's a lesbian' or 'This one hasn't had a man in weeks'. It made you want to curl up and die hearing stuff like that. It was nauseating. If we ever did anything wrong, the whole street had to know about it.

We children enjoyed our own company and did our work and went home. We got on very well together and were quite happy playing silly games as we walked home from school. Heather blindfolded me as I tried to walk without seeing and we smoked rolled up paper towels with leaves in them. We didn't play like normal kids. We'd go to derelict houses in the docks and chase rats.

We were always desperate for money and often cut up the back of the sofa to get any loose change that had fallen down the sides. We didn't pay for anything if we could help it.

We had guinea pigs at one point. We had to go out with Dad on a Sunday and run across a field to steal a bale of hay. The three of us kids ran like crazy and threw it into the back of Dad's van. He would syphon off some poor bloke's petrol on the way back home. It was Dad's idea and he built the hutch, but they were always breeding. One day they all died and Mum said she'd had enough of them anyway and that they stank so she and Dad burnt the cage.

Dad would always boast about finding cash in the street. He was lucky like that. He found £250 in an envelope once and needless to say he didn't for one moment think of handing it in to the police. He'd walk on the edge of the pavement looking in the gutter for cash. Looking back, I'm not so sure he found the money, I think it might have been the victims'.

Mum paid all the bills including the mortgage with Dad simply handing over his wage packet each week. He didn't even have a bank account. They just had Mum's Co-op one. When we were all at home Mum would easily spend £100 a week on food. She was a good cook and we were always well fed. There was roast dinner every Sunday and cakes afterwards.

We did a fair bit of the cooking. Dad was horrendous. He didn't have a clue. He bought six boxes of 'knock off' pork pies which we ate non stop until there were none left. He did lumpy mash to go with them. I begged him to let me cook because he was so bad. He got nasty if you didn't eat your the pies and in the morning you'd find it was fried up again for breakfast. We'd pretend to go to the loo and flush the food away or give it to the cat.

We were never allowed any friends to stay with us and we weren't allowed to stay with them. They wanted the family kept really tight. I hung around a lot with my sister Heather. We went through a lot together and understood each other. She'd land me in trouble at school because she smoked and I didn't, but I didn't mind.

Stephen...

I didn't have many friends for the simple reason Mum told them to fuck off when they came to the door. They never came to our house again, and you couldn't blame them. She answered the phone by saying 'What' and nothing else. Then someone would say something and she would say 'OK' and slam the phone down. She never said goodbye or anything like that.

She was so rude it was funny, like a Basil Fawlty comedy routine only ten times as vicious. I remember one time when she was looking around this electricity shop for a fridge when one of the assistants came over and asked 'Can I help you?' Mum replied 'Is there a law against looking?' She continued walking around this shop opening the doors of all the fridges and kicking them shut again. She bought the one that closed best with a kick.

I'd hate going shopping with her—you always knew something was going to happen. She'd think nothing of going into a clothes shop and trying to tear off the sleeves of sweaters. If she could do it she'd shout out 'Rubbish'. The same happened with shoes, but this time she'd rip off the soles. These were her tests of quality. Shops were left like war zones. Mum never used changing rooms. Clothes were whipped off in front of customers. It was embarrassing for us, but she didn't give a damn.

She wore this bobble hat with scarf and gloves when she went shopping in the winter. I used to say 'Mum, you can't go out in the street with that hat on' and her reply would be 'If you don't fucking like it—you shouldn't fucking look at me'. You didn't get in her way when she went round shops with a trolley. She raced round stores like Nigel Mansell. If you got in her way she'd run you over.

Mae...

Both Mum and Dad were completely unaware of how other people behaved. Everything they did was in a ramshackle way.

When we went on holiday they always stuck out. Dad would never have bothered to take us all away, but Mum nagged him and nagged him. She loves camping and so he agreed to go. It was really to give Mum a break and she didn't sleep with other men on holiday. We went seven years on the trot to Barry Island, a holiday camp in Wales. We'd travel up in Dad's transit van. The journeys were a nightmare because there were no seats in the back, just carpet. Most of us kids sat on the wheel arches. After a couple of hours in the back of the van we'd pull over at the side of the road and stretch our legs. We must have looked a right sight, all these kids jumping out of the back of a van.

It was always raining in Barry Island. You knew you were approaching Wales because you could see the rain clouds.

It's quite nice as seasides go, pebble beach and all that. Mum thought they were nice, friendly people there. We'd find a spot on the beach and then walk down to the pier and the shops but we'd never spend any money, all we did was look. But it was just like a home from home; all the rules still applied and we had to behave ourselves. We were never given pocket money at any age and never asked. We knew they had no money for us.

We'd paddle, walk round a bit and do things like bury each other in the sand. Dad and Mum never joined in the fun. The sea was usually freezing cold and we'd keep our costumes on under our clothes so we could have a dip when we wanted without having to change. We never had deckchairs because you had to pay for them. We sat on towels in the sand.

We had sandwiches which Mum had made for lunch but there were never enough to go round. I remember we'd have one each. Mum and Dad shared a flask of tea between us and we'd have squash which would be watered down with a lot of water. You could hardly taste the juice.

Sometimes we'd go and visit Dad's family at the farm in Much Marcle and we'd play with our cousins while the grown-ups talked. I remember going to Longleat Safari Park, which for us was a real treat. One of my sisters would sit between Mum and Dad in the front of the van while the rest of us hid under blankets in the back so Dad didn't have to pay the full entrance fee. Dad didn't know anything about the animals but he was fascinated by their breeding and got excited when he saw them having sex. On occasions he commented to us about it, but we didn't take any interest. He'd go on about their testicles. To us it was weird sex stuff, and meant nothing.

Holidays were never much good and even, if it was possible, went downhill when we bought a four-berth caravan. We had to clean it out before we went away in it, which wasn't all that often. A camping site in Shropshire called the Craven Arms was their favourite place to go. There was nothing on the site and to us it was really boring. Us kids went for long walks, we made our own fun.

Dad and Mum never played any games with us. Myself, Heather and Stephen played rounders or walked for miles and miles down lanes creating our own nature trail. We would talk and play and dance through the woods. Mum and Dad looked after the younger children and left us alone to do what we liked. We loved the countryside but then we had no choice, we couldn't go to any of the fairgrounds because there was no money.

Stephen and I once made the mistake of taking some friends we had made back to our caravan. It was about 10pm and the younger children were in the van with Mum and Dad. As we got closer to the caravan we could see it moving, sort of shaking. We quickly realised Mum and Dad were having sex, so we told our friends we had got lost and our caravan wasn't over there after all.

We didn't tell them that we weren't even sleeping in a caravan but Dad's van. There was no room in the caravan for all of us. One of the children had to sleep by the cooker because it was so cramped. Another couple of them were by the fridge. They were like sardines. Our blankets were chucked out on the floor for us to use as bedding. Dad made this table and chairs to fit inside the van and we'd sleep on a gangplank type of bed. It was the hardest thing you could imagine to sleep on. It was really fiddly trying to use the bed so we often didn't bother and slept on a chair or the table. It was pretty hopeless and very uncomfortable but most of all, it was freezing in the night. In the morning people would be getting their water for the day and stare at us in amazement in the van.

It was all a bit like a Carry On film but without the jokes. On one caravan site we were really embarrassed by them, even more than usual. We'd been out exploring and had returned back at about 10pm when I said 'What's that noise?' Our caravan was about 200 metres away and we heard this screaming as if someone was in agony. The noise got louder and louder as we got closer to our caravan. Everybody was standing around wondering what on earth was going on. People were looking out of their caravans and probably thinking someone was dying. Then we realised; it was Mum and Dad doing the business. They had the caravan windows open as well so it let all the noise out. And she sure didn't hold back.

We put our coats over our heads so that people wouldn't see us trying to get in the van. We just walked past them all at first. I couldn't believe it. Actually that was the first time we really said anything about it to Mum. You get a bit daring as you get older. We just said 'What was that noise last night?' and her response was 'Well, if you don't like it—go home. People don't have to listen, do they?' I told her she had a flaming audience outside. Last Night of the Proms!

We went to Snowdonia once and the wind blew the caravan over. Luckily we weren't in it at the time. In another place you weren't allowed to have a barbecue on the site so of course Dad had to have one. He set it up inside the awning and burnt it down. We were smoked out of the caravan.

You could never enjoy yourself with them, and as soon as us kids had a laugh ourselves, that was it, you got whacked. Mum thought nothing of saying 'stop bloody giggling' and then slapping us around the head with the back of her hand. This happened in the middle of the campsite with people watching. No one said anything. No one told her how to treat her kids. If they had tried Mum would have hung them out to dry. Mum's not very tall, but at about 5ft 4 and fourteen stone she's huge and the way she was built reflected her character. *Stephen...*

We never did anything different and never even went to the pub for coke and crisps. It was always the same year after year. Mum and Dad loved their routine, they couldn't think of behaving in any other way.

Funnily enough on holiday we didn't suffer any real abuse; that was always at home and never in public. Although holidays were never much fun we had an easy time as far as beatings were concerned. It was a relief to get out of the house and the neighbourhood.

We never mixed with Dad and Mum and to be honest it was relief to keep out of their way. They had the other kids to keep them busy, I suppose, and they created their own problems. There was the cooking, changing the gas bottles and trying to get the TV working. Dad still got up to his old tricks like pinching gas by swapping his empty bottle for a full one.

Mum and Dad were tight with money. Our five younger brothers and sisters started to get pocket money a few years ago because she's mellowed out a bit. Back then, if we wanted something like sweets we would ask her if we could do any extra jobs for her, like cleaning the windows, or clearing the back garden. You always had to ask first. A lot of the time she simply said 'no' and that was it. Only rarely did she say 'OK, you can do that for something'. All my friends got pocket money every week.

There was never any joy in our lives, it simply didn't exist. At the time it meant nothing. But now I think to myself 'How come you never took us out or something'. I was envious of an ex-girlfriend whose parents were always taking her out for a meal. It would have been the most bizarre thing in the world to ever happen to us, for my Dad to say 'let's go out for a meal', unheard of, unthinkable.

If Mum had said to me 'I love you' before we went to sleep I think I would have fainted, I'd have been sure she was on something.

We knew all along there was no Father Christmas. How? Mum told us—'He doesn't exist'. We were allowed one Christmas present. There was no magic about it, though. We'd be asked what we wanted then she'd get out the Argos catalogue and we were allowed to choose one present as long as it didn't cost more than £10. You knew what you were getting, which rather took the fun out of it. At least she wrapped the present up. What made us feel bad was that Mum couldn't even be happy at Christmas. She'd still be shouting and bawling.

Birthdays were funny. One year you got something and the next you didn't. You wouldn't get a card. I wouldn't mind, but we saved up between us to buy Mum and Dad a present every year.

Mae...

As kids we tried not to take too much notice of what Mum and Dad were up to. We were more interested in tying blankets to our beds and climbing out of the sash windows to climb down the front of the house. Dad wasn't upset about us hanging outside the house which, looking back, was a pretty silly and dangerous thing to do. He was more upset about us bouncing around on our beds and the rumblings below. He threatened us with a belting, but in the end he didn't do anything.

I was glad to get out the house and go to school, where life was normal to an extent. We would have been treated like any other kids if Mum hadn't dressed myself and Heather like boys. It was so bad we packed another set of clothes and shoes in a bag and changed as soon as we got outside the house. We certainly weren't popular and were always being picked on. I got teased about my name, which was like the month May until I changed it to Mae. They'd chant my name saying May, June, July.

I can't say I had many friends. It didn't help when Dad picked us up from school in something which looked like an ice cream van. Heather became very withdrawn at school and was always in trouble. I used to hang around her in what was called the smokers' corner when she had a few crafty fags.

Stephen was pretty average at school and wasn't particularly liked either. At the end of the day we waited for each other and walked home. We used to quite enjoy it.

Stephen was always getting into trouble of one kind or another and once, when we were walking home, he had a knife put to his throat. Someone in a car asked him for directions and then put a knife to his throat. Nothing happened, and we ran off.

After doing our homework we watched a bit of telly. Dad

wouldn't let us watch EastEnders because he said it was depressing. He banned us from watching quite a few programmes he didn't like himself. He said that *all* soap operas were depressing and that if we watched them then we'd have the wrong attitude for going to school. I used to go to my room and watch EastEnders hoping he wouldn't catch me.

When I was doing my mock 'O' level exams I couldn't do the necessary amount of studying because Mum had all these clients round. I had to mind the children and make them their tea. And when Dad got home from work I had to cook him something like scrambled egg on toast.

Mum made sure he had three set meals each day. When we were younger, she made home-made pies and cakes. When she didn't have much money, we had chunks of dried bread with hot milk on them. We also drank Bovril. If she couldn't afford to buy us all a chocolate bar, she'd slice it into eight pieces. A rare treat was fish and chips on a Saturday, but we always had some sort of Sunday meal.

Dad wouldn't let us girls shave for some reason, and was very strict about it. We sneaked Dad's razor from the bathroom cupboard by putting it up our sleeves. It was always tricky putting it back before he noticed. He caught us once and said we'd catch a disease if we shaved again. Of course we took no notice of what he was saying.

Chapter 4
Beatings

Stephen...

My first memory of being beaten was when I was about four or five.

Dad was really quiet at times but he snapped very quickly. It was more abusive than violent—he used to threaten us by saying 'I'll fucking kill you, you bastard'. He was vicious when he got angry. His eyes would roll and he would be livid. He was the same as my mum, but he didn't flip as often. Mum was like that every other day. Dad would flip once a year, but when he did go he was like a madman.

The worst times were when he punched me. There was never a reason for him to go so crazy. We played up like any kids, but we weren't bad. I didn't drink, smoke or take drugs. I did my homework and I was good at school. There was no reason for any of it.

The slightest thing would set Mum off. When I was young we had turf all over the back garden and it would get very muddy in the winter. I would walk back into the house and maybe leave a little bit of mud on the carpet. Well, Mum would blow up like a volcano. I would try to run away but she would catch me and give me a good hiding. There was never a time when you'd do something wrong and not get hit. It was never 'go to your bedroom' or anything like that.

47

Mum had no self-control. She would just flip and have no real idea what she was doing. I used to scream, always scream. I felt so helpless, especially when Mum was hitting my sisters. I would stand there and just watch. I wanted to help them, I really did.

Mum would hit out with anything she could lay her hands on. She wasn't terribly choosy. If she'd had a sledgehammer in her hands she would have belted you with it. A rolling pin was one of her favourites. She would just lash out and you'd be sent flying.

We had a table about two-and-a-half feet high dividing the kitchen from the living room. We would sit at the table on stools, wooden ones, with big metal legs. I shouted back at Mum once, which was always a bad move to make, and Mum just picked up one of the stools up and flung it at me. Luckily, I ducked and it missed me.

One day I had, as usual, done something wrong and was washing the kitchen floor. We had a mop but she told me 'Get on your hands and knees and do it with a cloth,' so I was on my hands and knees with a bowl, scrubbing the floor. She climbed on a stool to put something on the shelf. I moved the bowl as I was cleaning and then she stepped down—right into the bowl of water. I didn't laugh, I just looked at the floor and waited. I knew what to expect. She turned round and took her foot out the water and the next thing I knew she'd smashed the bowl straight over my head. She hit me as hard as she possibly could. It didn't bleed because I was hit with the flat base of the bowl. I've still got the lump on my head.

I was dazed and when my head cleared she was kicking me and swearing and shouting: 'You did that on purpose, you little swine'. She boasted about the beating to Dad when he got home. 'I had to beat him across the head with a bowl,' she said. 'You won't forget it—will you?' Then she started laughing at me and Dad joined in.

There was one beating which will always stick in my mind. Mum rang up my school and said: 'I want my son home straight away.' The teacher told me and, thinking someone had been badly hurt, I rushed home.

I opened the door and saw Mum and she was really calm. I couldn't understand it. She told me to go into the bathroom, strip off and shut the door. I thought it was a bit strange, though I imagined she wanted me to shower or something. I looked round and saw this belt and wire hanging up and I thought 'What have I done wrong now?'

She told me to put my hands together, and tied the wire round my wrists. Then she told me to lie on the floor and put my hands around the bottom of the toilet. They were then tied to the base of the toilet so I couldn't move. I couldn't understand what was going on. I was naked and felt pathetic. I knew that I hadn't done anything wrong and I felt total fear.

Mum looked so pleased with herself. She was completely calm as she tied my feet together. It was really chilling, horrible. She got the belt down and stood on my legs and said: 'Right then, what have you done wrong, son?' I said: 'Nothing, Mum. I haven't done anything.' She said I had taken something that morning, and started whacking me.

She continued for about twenty minutes. She wouldn't tell me what I was supposed to have done. I don't think it would have made any difference if she had told me and I had said she was wrong. She kept whacking me with the belt, always the buckle end and never the straps, and she aimed it at the base of my spine. I was screaming as she whacked me and kicked me.

She kept shouting out: 'What have you done wrong? What have you done wrong?' That's all she kept saying. She was good at repeating things, like a stuck record. She looked so happy, so pleased with herself.

I was screaming, really screaming, but there was no-one else in the house to hear me. Then she said: 'Right, I'll tell you what you've done. You stole some magazines from upstairs' and I said 'No, I haven't. I swear to God I haven't.' I kept saying 'I haven't' and she started hitting me again. Then she stopped, put the belt round her waist and did it up.

She went out of the room for about ten minutes, then she came back and untied me. She told me, in a really nice, sickly sweet voice, to get dressed and go back to school. She was so cold, so bloody cold and unfeeling. I was bleeding, but it didn't show through the black trousers I put on. I was cut around the bottom and around the backs of my legs and at the base of my spine.

Mum had kept kicking me in the stomach, so I was bruised all over. She told me to 'tell them at school one of your sisters has been hurt'. I was crying so much on my way back to school that I had to go into the toilets and wash my face. I went back into the class and said: 'Sorry, my mum needed me at home'.

I told Mae on the way back from school what had happened and she couldn't believe it. I went through the front door at exactly the same time as my older sister Heather arrived home. Heather gave Mum this note from her school saying they had confiscated some sex magazines from her. Heather was really worried she was going to get told off but Mum just said: 'Don't worry, Stephen got your beating.' She laughed and carried on making the tea. Heather felt really guilty. I was glad Mum didn't hit her as well.

Dad came home from work and we were all doing the chores. Even though I'd been given a beating for something I didn't do, she still treated me terribly. She told Dad everything and then turned to me and said 'Didn't I, son?' and I said 'What ?' and she said 'Didn't I give you a good beating?' and I replied 'Yeah', and Dad just laughed. They were laughing together.

I felt totally degraded. My mum had beaten me when I was naked and made me feel so feeble. I tried to be good to Mum—to make her like me—but it didn't work, ever. She would ignore me for ages and I would try to make it up, rather stupidly really. I wanted to talk to her again so I was no longer in trouble and in her bad books. I never got a sorry. She has never said sorry to me to this day.

By far the worst experience I had as a child, and there were a few, was when I was about twelve years old. I made the mistake, if you can call it that, of sitting on some units which had arrived. Mum told me to get down, and I did as I was told. But, by mistake, I sat on them again. I don't know why—I was just a kid.

Mum was carrying something, but she stopped and slowly put it down, before turning to look at me. She grabbed my arm and pulled me into the living room. With one hand she tugged at my neck and with the other she was trying to take my jeans down. Mum's hand was crushing my neck, as I was only small.

She was shouting to my sister to pull my trousers down for her because she couldn't get them down with one hand. I was struggling to try to get away. My sister started crying as she didn't want to do it and Mum then attacked her, shouting at her, saying: 'I'll hit you as well if you don't.' She then held my neck with her two hands clasped tightly around it and lifted me off the ground. She held me there for at least 5 minutes with just her hands round my neck. I could hardly breathe and I felt dizzy. I was groaning but she wasn't taking any notice.

My sister was screaming and crying and Mum told her to take my trousers off at once or she would get it as well. I kept blacking out and then coming round again. I was in a right mess. For a minute I thought I'd had it—there was nothing I could do at all. Everything kept going dark and I just thought I wasn't going to wake up in a minute. The more I tried to get away, the tighter she put her hands around my neck.

Then Dad walked in from somewhere and she just dropped me on the floor and walked away. Dad didn't say anything. He looked at me and then walked back out with Mum.

For two weeks, I had her fingerprints on my neck. I had to cover them up before I went to school with my shirt collar and tie. She gave me a note for school which said I was fooling around in a tree with a rope and then I fell out and that's how I got spots on my forehead and in my eyes. The blood vessels in my eyes had burst. All I remember is going to see the headmaster and that was the end of it. My school mates took the mickey out of me when I told them I had done it tying a rope round my neck. It was a lot safer not to tell the truth.

I should have gone to the doctors, really, but Mum wouldn't let me go. I was worried because I could hardly speak. I couldn't speak at all for a day, and then I spoke in a really high-pitched voice.

I made sure I didn't cross Mum for a long time after that little incident. I made sure I did everything right, and I tried to be good so she would forgive me. I used to deliberately get home from school as quickly as I could, get changed without saying anything, and do housework and any extra work that needed doing.

After it happened, I didn't speak to Mum for ages and she wouldn't speak to me. We didn't go near each other. I was embarrassed and thought it was all my fault. When someone does something like that, someone really close to you like your parents, for some strange reason it's embarrassing to face them afterwards. I don't know why. With our parents we weren't used to them being nice or apologising for what they had done.

We tried very hard not to put ourselves in a position where they might feel they should be pleasant to us. I remember Dad saying sorry for punching me one time. It was horrible, because I didn't like the idea of him feeling sorry for me. Not that Mum ever was. She never said sorry or showed any regrets. She would just laugh.

Once when I was eating some eggs for dinner I left the yolk. When Mum had her back turned I put it in the bin. I went out to play and she called me back in, grabbed me round the neck, took me to the bin and said: 'Did you put that in there?' and I said no because it wasn't smart to admit to anything. She said: 'Yes, you did, now eat it.' It was covered in rubbish from the bin, the slops, everything. She made me get a fork and eat it out of the bin in front of her. I felt as sick as a dog afterwards. It was vile.

If you upset Mum at the dinner table, if you were talking too much, she'd slap you round the head. If you didn't eat your dinner, you weren't allowed to get down from the table. I remember my two sisters sitting there for three hours until they ate the rest of their cold meal.

All my mates were scared of her. No-one knocked on the door to ask if I was coming out to play. My mate Mark did it once. When she opened the door, he said: 'Is Steve there?' and she replied 'Why?' and he said: 'I want him to come out' and without a moment's thought she answered 'You're fucking joking,' and shut the door in his face. He never came back again. He was terrified. She used to say: 'Don't come round here, my kids have got work to do, and none of my kids spend their life on the street.' Unless you had an argument with her of course, and you left home, and she couldn't give a shit.

It was always Mum who would hand out the beatings, and rarely Dad. He used to work such long hours he was never there. It was quite rare to see both my parents together. Dad would be working, and when he got home Mum would be with her men friends upstairs. He would go back to work, and then she would come down. I don't think Dad was that bothered about us really. Neither of them kissed or cuddled us at all. Later, when we were much older and had younger brothers and sisters, they kissed Dad before they went to bed, and sometimes Mum if she was around.

I don't think Dad wanted me to be like him. He never wanted me to work with him doing jobs around the house. I had to beg him. When he worked for his building boss, Derek, he felt threatened if someone could do something he couldn't do. I was fixing my sister's bike one day and he told me to leave it until he came home and then he'd sort it out. I was bored that day so I thought I'd do him a favour and fix it before he got home. But when he got back later and he saw the bike had been repaired he lost it. 'Who the bloody hell told you to fix it?,' he shouted. Then without saying another word he punched me straight on the side of the jaw, knocked out my back tooth, and walked away.

I ran to get out the back door but Mum locked it before I got

there. Dad came running after me and began punching and kicking me. A girlfriend told the Social Services what had happen and they said Mum and Dad could be prosecuted for what they had done. But I said no, and that was the end of that.
Mae...

When I was about eight or nine I was getting changed once in my vest and knickers and Mum was cutting meat in the kitchen. She was shouting at usual. For some reason she picked on me and came at me with a knife. I was sitting there on the top step in the lounge and she came towards me. She flashed at me with the knife. I was crying and said 'no, Mum, no Mum, no Mum'. She kept slashing the knife at me and there were little nicks all over my rib cage. I was crying and quite terrified.

You never knew what Mum was going to do next. It was scary and I suppose something you came to expect. I've got no scars, she just nicked me. She could be nasty and violent for no real reason. It lasted seconds, but I'll never forget it.
Stephen...

I hated seeing my sisters or brothers hurt in any way. It really got to me seeing Mae crying and bathing the nicks in her skin in the bathroom.

It was all one way traffic, there was no thanks for anything, no good words or pats on the back. I would say to Mae and Heather 'Why doesn't she bloomin' well thank us for what we do?' Somehow Mum got to know what we were talking about and took us aside to tell us: 'The day I've got to thank my kids for cleaning our house is the day they get out.'

One day, after a particularly bad beating from both my parents, I ran to my girlfriend's home and stayed there for a couple of days because I was too scared to go back home. I went to school the next day as usual and my girlfriend told one of the teachers, who called the Social Services. I wouldn't talk to them, though, as I was too scared in case it got me into more trouble. They never contacted Mum and Dad, and even if they had, there was nothing they could do. Mum and Dad wouldn't have changed if the Pope had knocked on the door and said: 'Treat your kids better.' They would have told him to fuck off as well.

Funnily enough, none of all this made any real impression on us as children. It's what you got used to, it was normal life. We knew no different. All we thought was that these were Mum's and Dad's moods and tempers.

We were tough kids and looked after each other because of what we went through. We saw the other children getting hit for something as trivial as not eating all their tea. Mum would whack you round the head if you said you couldn't eat everything.

She wore Dad's leather belt all the time because it was one of her weapons. It was two inches wide and made of crisscrossed leather. She would drag you down from the table by your neck and beat you loads of times and then throw you back onto the table. She boasted about how she would never hit us on the backside because it never hurt there. Her favourite target was across the base of the spine, where she would whip you with the buckle. The pain brought tears to your eyes. I think it was a sexual thing with Mum.

I remember one time when I was five and Mae was six and Heather would have been seven. We were down in the basement where we slept when we were young. It wasn't very nice down there at all. A prison cell would have been an improvement, but we were put down there because our parents wanted peace, or that's what they told us. Dad heard us talking and he and Mum marched down to sort us out. They grabbed the three of us, dressed only in our nightclothes, and chucked us outside the front door.

It was raining, and we stood there in our bare feet in pyjamas and nightclothes. All we had done wrong was talk when we should have been asleep. And this was our punishment. We were outside for over fifteen minutes. I've never been so cold in my life. We cuddled up together using our body heat to help each other. We thought we were in the wrong and probably deserved it.

It was gone ten o'clock when we were let in, because I remember counting the chimes of the church clock and then we were put to bed.

Whatever you did wrong Mum gave you a good slapping. She thought nothing of kicking you. There was never any rhyme nor reason to it. I think she used to get off on hitting us. She openly admits she did it.

Mae ....

We were so scared of her when she was younger because she was really nasty. She'd hit one of us and then she'd want to hit us all because she was in the mood. We'd all have to hide in our rooms and wait until she calmed down. I think she just lost control.

She eased off when I was fifteen and that was the last time she hit me. She's been an absolutely brilliant mother since. A lot of times I said when I was fifteen it would be the last time she'd ever hit me because after that I'd do something about it.

We have never spoken out or asked her why she did it. I don't mention it now, it's as if it never happened. Mum has admitted to me: 'I know I was nasty when I was younger but I had a lot of problems'. I left it at that.

Stephen...

I can't say I ever understood Dad and I don't think he gave a damn about understanding me. I'd watch him when he was thinking, whilst he was watching the telly. He really used to stare at it when the news was on, and we weren't allowed to talk to him.

At times when you least expected it, he'd completely flip. The second before he could be as happy as Larry, then suddenly he would hit the roof. It wasn't like normal anger. His eyes rolled and he became really, really scary.

There was one time when Mum and Dad did actually look after me—though only because a policeman told them to. It was the first time I ever drank. A few mates made a cocktail for me down at the park. I didn't know quite what it was, but they put everything in it like aspirins, paracetamol and cider. I drank the whole bottle and was absolutely out of my head, blotto. I was dancing in the road. It was the time when skinheads were out in force and I saw a whole load of them coming down the street. I was shouting out 'fuck you' so they attacked me, about fifteen of them. All I saw was this size 12 Doc Martin boot coming into my face, then it all went blank from then on.

Apparently they threw me in a brook and, luckily for me, a policeman found me half dead, face down in the water. He dragged me out, took me to hospital and called my Dad to tell him what had happened. The policeman said: 'I will let you have him on one condition—you look after him all night.' Dad agreed, threw me over his shoulder and took me home. Mum sat with me through the night.

Mae...

Funnily enough, the only times Mum and Dad were good to us was when we were in trouble with the police. Me, Stephen and about nine school mates were bored one day and while walking home together thought: 'Let's do over W.H. Smith.'

Stephen...

We never got any new things, and the only way we were going to get our hands on this stuff was to steal it. We had these big black plastic bags and put everything in them we could get our hands on. We took books, pencils and colouring books, before we were caught. I was only ten at the time and thought if I cried a lot we could get away with it.

Mae...

The manager was horrible and the police were called. They took us away in a police van with our shoes and socks taken off so we couldn't run away. We stood in this cell waiting for Mum and Dad to come and get us. Mum and Dad were fine about it. We didn't get into any trouble. We got banned from seeing our friends, that was all. We were below the criminal age so the police couldn't do anything to us. The school found out about it and we got into trouble with them.

If you'd have killed someone and you wanted them to hide the gun, our parents would probably have done it for you. They would do anything for us if we'd done something illegal.

Stephen...

Dad could be really funny at times, though not in the way most people would think was funny. He once smashed a light bulb over Mae's head, one of the big fluorescent tubes, eight foot long ones. He was swinging it over her head and then he smacked it across her ear and it exploded, all across the living room.

Mae...

It didn't hurt and I was laughing so much Mum thought I was crying. He told everyone about it and it used to really embarrass me.

Stephen...

You could have a great laugh at times—it wasn't all gloom and doom. But the fun was always at someone else's expense.

All Dad wanted to do was boss me. He liked to think he had complete power over the house and that everyone answered to him. When Dad was at home, that was it, he took over. When Dad wasn't there, Mum was in control.

He used to order her around when we were young kids, but I don't remember him ever hitting her. They messed around with each other and played rough, that was all. They used to argue a bit, though not that much. I found it strange how well they got on really, like two peas in a pod.

When Dad hit me, I never reacted. I never, ever, hit him back. But not long before he was arrested, things changed. Dad didn't approve of me seeing other girls when I had this serious relationship with Andrea. He liked Andrea and this was before we got married. He said to me: 'I'll tell Andrea what you're really like. What you're really up to.'

I told him to shut his mouth and walked away. He said 'You don't tell me to shut my mouth' and he pulled me back and punched me on the jaw. Then for the first time in my life I whacked him back. I felt guilty afterwards. I smacked him in the mouth, and because I was wearing a ring I smashed up his lip and gum. He kept hitting me, and we were fighting for over twenty minutes, just punching. I couldn't believe what I was doing but I couldn't stop myself.

Finally he said 'Let's stop this' and we did. He was really

shaking and then he looked me in the eyes and said: 'Look, I love you, I don't want this. I just love you and want you to make the best of your life.' He felt really guilty for fighting me.

I had really caught him with one blow and I thought to myself: 'Oh, God'. There was blood all over his mouth. Andrea stood rooted to the spot whilst all this was happening. She was totally shocked.

Dad was incredibly emotional and for once was sorry for trying to hurt me. That was the first time he had shown real feeling towards me. I don't know whether it was me hitting him back that did it or whether he knew the past was going to catch up with him sooner or later and he didn't want us to fall out forever.

From then on he treated me like an angel, like a man, a proper man. He let me do things he had never let me do before, he trusted me. If we were on a job together in the past he'd always wanted to do the dangerous bits. But now he felt I could look after myself.

I do feel bitter about my childhood. Yet it hasn't left any scars, it was just the way it was. I'm glad I'm here now and I survived it all.

Nothing was ever straight forward. Like when I left home they had to be completely and utterly callous. I was fifteen and Mum decided that she'd had enough of me living at home, so she told me that I had to move out. Two days later she'd found me a bedsit and made all the kids grab a piece of my stuff and marched us down the road like an army of soldier ants.

My stuff was dumped in the room and they all marched off leaving me on my own. It was: 'Get out, here's your stuff, and don't come back unless it's for an hour on a Sunday.' I could look after myself, but I cried for three weeks. I felt so alone all of a sudden. I wasn't even allowed to make a cup of tea when I did pay a visit.

I feel cheated now. I suppose I felt cheated at the time, but you just accepted it over the years. It's only when I compare my life with people the same age that I think there was something seriously wrong. When I went out with my first girlfriend I compared my life with hers—and it made me think. I saw her and her friends as spoilt rather than being brought up properly. I remember I used to be envious of my friends because they used to stay at each others houses. I was never allowed to stay out unless I ran away. You then got your stuff thrown out behind you and they would say: 'Go on then, sling your hook.'

When I used to run away I had every intention of not coming back again, but after a couple of weeks on the streets, it was hard. Dad never came to look for me and I knew they didn't really care if I was dead or alive. When I came home, they'd be watching TV together and they wouldn't look twice at me. Then you knew you were in for a beating, that was obvious, and then life carried on.

The last few weeks before Dad was arrested, he encouraged me to make something of my life and treated me properly. He wanted me to do a proper carpentry course so I had some qualifications and could start my own business and make some money. It was almost like he sensed he was going. He once showed me the route to a big DIY merchants, and I didn't remember how to get there so we went there five times. Then he asked me to drive and I went straight there. 'Don't forget,' he told me 'I might not be here one day, so I want you to remember everything I have told you'. He knew it was a matter of time. I think he knew Heather's disappearance was never going to be laid to rest until she was found.

Mae...

When I left school I wanted my own life. Mum and Dad basically kicked me out when I was sixteen; I had a boyfriend called Rob Williams and they pushed us to move in together. We'd only been going out for three weeks, but he'd been staying at Cromwell Street. I was quite frightened. I wasn't sleeping with Rob, and after the closeness of the family, it seemed strange to be out on my own. Mum and Dad said I could only come round on a Sunday and I had to hand back the keys to the house.

The rent was pretty much the same cost as a mortgage, so my boyfriend and I decided to buy a house together. His parents gave us the money for the deposit and we bought a fairly new house in a nice part of town. Mum and Dad wouldn't even come round. Dad said I should have bought a house in Cromwell Street and made part of it into bedsits, so we could have made some money.

I was really proud of the house and wanted them to see how well I'd done for myself, so I had to con them into coming round. I told them there was an electrical problem and urgently needed help. All they did was mock the place when they did eventually turn up. They said the house was so small it was like a rabbit hutch. 'You could have got a house in Cromwell Street for the same money,' they said.

They wouldn't let any of the other children come and see me. It really hurt to think they were more interested in controlling my life than helping me.

I have asked Mum about all the violence and why she did it, but she plays it down. I think she's a bit ashamed of it, but she did have eight kids and a husband like Dad, so it's not surprising she was so stressed. I don't think she'll ever admit how hard she was. I don't feel bitter about it now. We get on brilliantly, but I think she was wrong and I try to forgive her.

When I was older I said to myself I never wanted to live like my family, I want to be normal. But maybe I don't know what normal is.

I dream of being a successful career woman. I've got five 'O' levels but Mum and Dad wouldn't let me take 'A' levels. I told Dad about my exams and he said 'You don't want exams, you're going to have babies'.

Dad never had any confidence in women to do anything. When I passed my driving test all he said to me was: 'There must be some mistake,' and it took him ages before he got in a car with me.

Mum and Dad said I had to get a job or else, not a career, but something to earn my keep. Even when I was earning £28 a week, I had to give Mum £10 a week.

I worked at a factory washing-up and I went to an evening business course. Then I worked at a big cinema complex where I was promoted from office junior to secretary. Dad said I should be concentrating on getting a husband and having babies. I was only sixteen.

Chapter 5
Sex

Stephen...

Dad saw sex in everything. Even if he was giving you a lift he'd say he'd seen someone having it in the woods or something. Every day he'd see a crash and claim his van was covered with blood, but we never saw any. Or he'd say a girl had run out at him waving her knickers in the air to try and stop him. Another time he'd say he'd picked up a hitchhiker who was 'begging for it'. He'd claim that she'd had her skirt hitched right up while he was trying to drive.

You could never get away from sex, and if he went for a walk in the park with the dogs he would see people at it on park benches. He was obsessed with sex. We used to make a joke about it with him, saying that he turned everything around to sex, and he would laugh. He thought everyone was the same as him.

I know he was sleeping with one of the victims, Shirley Robinson, who was a lodger. I didn't know her but I know he used to have sex with her a lot. He would leave Mum in bed at night and go and see Shirley and go back to Mum in the morning. That's what the police told me, and Dad backed it up.

About five years ago there were two gay women who lived in the street and Dad used to ask them around. They used to go upstairs into the middle front room where the bar is and do whatever they did with Mum and Dad. Dad said he hated lesbians, that they were too dry inside.

Dad was never discreet. Mum never wore underwear, and the first thing he did when he came home was to stick his dirty hand straight up her skirt and smell it. Right in front of us. Sometimes he would grab my hand and try to stick it up her skirt or my sister's. We were horrified by it all.

If a friend was there Dad would still do it. My girlfriend would be there and he would do it—people would just look away in total disbelief. We can laugh about it now, it's just a terrible shame we didn't realise the implications for Heather.

Our parents didn't care. They didn't give a damn. They didn't say: 'Oh, look away,' and try and do things where we couldn't see. It was like making a cup of tea for them. They wouldn't expect you to react at all.

I don't remember the first time I was conscious of it, it just grew into our lives. You never got used to that kind of thing happening. Every time you thought: 'Oh my God,' and felt really embarrassed.

When I brought a girlfriend, Nicola, home for the first time we were sitting in the living room waiting to meet Mum and she came downstairs in her dressing gown to have a shower. I called her and introduced her to Nicola, but she totally ignored us, didn't speak a word to Nicola. That was Mum all over.

After showering, she came out stark naked with the dressing gown in her hand and went straight upstairs. My girlfriend didn't know where to look. I was so embarrassed I just hung my head down. Mum didn't speak to her for three weeks.

She used to walk past my mates starkers as well. I had to tell them not to look. I remember when Mae's boyfriend was there, we were laying carpet and Mum just sat with her legs open. She had a skirt on with nothing on underneath and if we looked at her, there was nothing we couldn't see. She couldn't have cared less. Her attitude was: 'If they don't like what they see, they shouldn't be looking.' If I said: 'Don't do that in front of so and so,' Mum and Dad would say: 'Well don't bring her around again if she doesn't like it.'

It may sound strange but when you're living like that, it's just each day as it comes—you cope with it as it is. The thing was that every day was different in our house, something strange happened. You either got a new beating or you'd see a new bloke with Mum, or Dad would do a new weird thing.
Mae...

Dad was into experiments; inter-breeding and trying to make his own race. He used to play around with syringes and tried to artificially inseminate Mum. He advertised the fact that he could do abortions through his workmates and friends. Dad claimed that he was medically trained and used to boast about performing them. There were also a lot of medicine bottles and stuff about, which he used to pinch from somewhere.

There were a lot of strange things happening, but when Mum used to explain, it didn't sound so bad. Dad always took it to the limit. Like taking pictures with a zoom lens, he wanted to go right into the body and look at the internal organs. It was always like that with him.

I love cats, and years ago Mum gave me a really good cat book. Dad borrowed it. I didn't think he was interested, but he wanted it for the breeding section inside, and he would never give it back to me. He wanted to see if it was possible to play with things, to play about with nature. I know he talked about having cat runs in the back garden, like chickens, for breeding, but he never got around to doing anything about it. A lot of his ideas were kept between them, whispered or whatever, upstairs.

Stephen...

Dad always wanted to breed Mum with a bull. That's why they had bulls on each corner of their four poster bed. He used to say: 'The only thing that would satisfy you is a bull.' He said he was going to try to get her one to 'sort her out'. He had some blue movies which showed a woman performing oral sex on a horse and then having full intercourse with it. Then there was one with an Alsatian dog. I remember there was one picture of Mum in a car sitting on a gear stick. Dad was fascinated by it.

Mum and Dad used to put semen into test tubes and inject it into girls to see if they could make a baby out of it. At least that's what Dad said. Dad believed you could muck around genetically with people. I think in his own way he thought he could play God.

He had a thing about women's bodies—he was into internal bits—and he wanted to get as close as he could. He really wanted to get inside them. He'd think: 'I wonder what that looks like,' and have a look. I know he wanted a tiny little pencil camera, the ones they use on pregnant women. He wanted to look at the womb because it was something he didn't have.

I remember going upstairs looking for some paper and an envelope and I opened this drawer and it was full of sex toys—more than I had ever seen in my life. As a 12 year-old I knew about vibrators and stuff like that from school, and from the fact that it was so open in our house. But in the drawer were about 30 different things—dildos, whips, everything.

Sex

Mae...

Mum didn't really have any friends because Dad wouldn't allow it. And if she found someone to have a cup of tea with, Dad would throw them out of the house. He didn't really want her to talk to anyone else. He wanted complete power over the house. Everyone answered to him. When Dad was home, that was it, Dad took over. As soon as he came home it was 'I am here, I'm boss'.

In the corner of their bedroom were piles of porn magazines. Another time when Stephen and I were being nosy we found kinky rubber suits and masks under a mattress, and a lot of underwear. Some of it must have been mail order, but other stuff Mum must have bought at the shops.

My parents were strange people and I tried to think of the things that made them normal. When we found all that stuff, we put it down to them just doing their own thing.

They had loads of other blue films which Dad insisted on loaning to everyone, me, my boyfriend Rob, anyone. There was no way you could refuse, so we would take the videos for a couple of weeks and bring them back unwatched.

Dad told me once that he had hidden in a tree with his video camera filming Mum having sex in the back of his van when the back doors were open. I don't think the bloke knew he was being filmed, and Dad nearly fell out of the tree.

In the house, if he was listening to her on the intercom and she was laughing with the customer beforehand, or she wasn't smiling on the video of it, he'd shout at her. She couldn't do anything right. She had to pretend to the customer that she was having a good time. But if Dad thought she was really enjoying it then he'd go straight upstairs and punch her.

Dad would sometimes drive her over to houses to sleep with

men. He'd pretend to be her brother, and she would have to stay there all night. Sometimes she would either pretend to go in or leave after an hour, and then she'd sleep on a park bench and come home at 6am so that Dad wouldn't know what had happened. But sometimes she did stay over with a boyfriend. If she didn't do what Dad asked he'd say she was a bad mother and wife and that good wives should always do what their husbands said.

They had all sorts of sex aids piled into a black case which was full of dildos. He used to show us one he called the Eiffel Tower which he used to offer to lend my friends if they came round. He used to show us the other stuff as well. He also had a cat o' nine tails, which I remember seeing him make when I was about five or six. I didn't know what it was for then but years later I saw it in their bedroom. It was made out of strips of leather.

If I showed any friends around the house I made sure I shut the door before they saw the inscription on the bed. It was always embarrassing if Dad was there and he wanted to show them, because he used to say things to our friends and it would get round the school that my dad was a bit funny.

We looked up the word 'buggery' once in a dictionary because Dad had told Stephen that they used to do that. We didn't have a clue what he was talking about.

They didn't care where they had sex. I know the younger ones saw them doing it on the big table downstairs and in the kitchen. They just didn't care who saw them or how much noise they made.
Stephen...

But they wanted to be the ones who decided who saw what. Dad used to do the bingo and put the cards on the mantelpiece in his bedroom. One day I went up to put one there and accidentally walked in on Mum and a boyfriend having sex. I ran downstairs to the basement crying, and Dad just beat me saying I had wanted to watch and I deliberately walked in on them.

They did it all the time. I bought them a tent so they could go into parks and do it. It was one of their birthdays and I asked them what they would like. We guessed what it was for.

If Mae and I were there, we would go off on a walk with the dogs and make ourselves scarce. Before the tent they used to do it in the bushes! They both had high sex drives.

Mae...

Dad was a racist but he wanted black men to sleep with Mum—he thought they were well endowed. I think he made Mum feel cheap in bed with his quick legovers. I'm sure other men would give her more affection than Dad. She wanted more from him. He never used to take her out, although she wanted to go.

She didn't really want to go with other men, she wanted her husband. But he wanted her to sleep with other men—the bigger the better, and the blacker the better. He had a thing about size, and some of the sex equipment they had was huge. One black dildo he had was 14 inches long and he called it his 'cunt buster'. He was always referring to it and asking if we wanted to borrow it. We even found one of their vibrators, which they had obviously forgotten about, in an old fridge in the basement .

A few years ago, when there was a big AIDS scare around the world, Dad was convinced he had caught it. So he and Mum went for a test but it was clear. Mum said she had protected sex with the clients.

I know she was sterilised once and later changed her mind and asked the hospital to reverse the process. She did get pregnant again but I think she suffered a miscarriage.

Dad didn't believe that one man could produce so many children without there being something wrong with them. He believed that after a while you'd start having handicapped children, so he insisted on Mum sleeping with other men. But I think the reason he really made her do it was because he found it a really big turn-on.

Chapter 6
Abuse

Mae West was raped when she was eight years old. It left her deeply scarred and she blotted it out of her mind, suppressing all emotions for years before she was able to tell someone what had happened.

Mae...

I was playing happily in the garden when a visitor called me into the bathroom and locked the door behind me. He picked me up and put me on top of the babies' changing board which Dad had made to fit on top of the bath. It was big and covered half of the bath because that's where Mum did the nappies.

He made me lie down and tried to penetrate me. He didn't take his clothes off, he just unzipped himself. He didn't undress me, he just took off my knickers. I can't remember what he said or how I felt. I just remember what happened. I remember wriggling about, which made him annoyed. He told me: 'I can't do anything if you keep moving about.'

It was actual rape, penetration, and it lasted several seconds. How long exactly I don't know. I suppose I was just trying to fight him off and eventually he opened the door and I went out. It was during the school holidays because I know Stephen and

Heather were in the house but I didn't go to them afterwards.

I remember he smelt of cigars. I don't like cigar smoke. Whenever someone smokes cigars near me, it reminds me of him.

Afterwards he came up to me and started talking about money. He threw a 10 pence at me and told me not to tell anyone, it was just between him and me or something.

I didn't cry, I know that. I suppose it must have been painful but I have blocked it out of my mind. Whenever I think about it, I think of it as someone else, so I don't feel any emotions about it. I didn't tell anyone about what happened until I was about 14 and went swimming with my half sister Anne-Marie.

I couldn't have told my parents because we were engulfed in sex from an early age. It was everywhere around the house and that was the norm. They probably would have said: 'Well, that's so and so, it's alright,' so I just forgot it. I think that was the best way. Anyway, I didn't want them saying I was lying or making it up, so I have never told my mum even to this day.

The police found out recently and made me make a statement, but I have told them I will never go to court and give evidence. If he starts denying it, I think that would really hurt me. It just seems so long ago. I've cut it out so much I sometimes even think it didn't happen at all. But I couldn't have made it up.

There were visitors to the house all the time, and Heather and I used to get touched up regularly. Dad was the worst. His whole life revolved around sex. Everything he said would boil down to it. Even if you were talking about the weather he would end up talking about sex.

He wanted to know how often people were doing it and to whom. Anyone who came round to visit or anyone who he'd known for a couple of minutes, he would ask about their sex life.

Whenever he met a woman he would say they wanted him badly, he could tell. One of my aunties got so fed up and didn't come round again. A lot of people stopped coming.

Sex had to be every night or he'd think Mum didn't love him. We used to hear them when we were kids and he used to tell us about his sex life. He'd come down in the morning and say: 'I had your mother last night.'

He would put things in the crudest way and I suppose we got used to it. He'd say 'I had a good ride last night' or 'I screwed the arse off her'. As we got older I would say: 'We don't want to know, Dad,' and a lot of the time I would blank it out. Then he would say to Stephen: 'You'll soon be ready to sleep with your mum,' and Mum and Dad would laugh.

Stephen...

When Dad said something like that, I just ignored him and let it wash over my head. I know he would have liked it if I had shown some interest, but I don't think he would have tried to force me.

Mae...

It was really bad for me and Heather when we reached puberty, at about 12 or 13. Dad used to comment on our breast size or how they had grown a bit. He thought, if he created his daughter he should be able to look at his creation and touch it. He said a father's right is to break his daughters in and it was his privilege to do it by the time we were 16. According to him, that was what his father had done.

He also used to say he wanted us to have his baby. He'd say: 'Your first baby should be your Dad's.' He said if we got pregnant we could hand the baby over to Mum. I don't know why. He reckoned we would just be able to call it our brother or sister.

He thought he was an expert on anything sexual. We had to almost parade in front of him. He said things like: 'Why don't you come out of the bathroom without the towel on?' If we wrapped one around us he would try and rip it off so he could see us naked. We used to peep out of the door, see where he was, and then run to our room and try and get our clothes on as quickly as possible.

He got mad if I covered myself up in the shower. If he heard me in there he would put his hands around the shower curtain and touch me. He never said anything while he was doing it. He didn't feel he had to make excuses or justify it. He felt it was his right. He didn't see himself as a paedophile, he just saw it as natural, natural to see what he had produced.

He'd get nasty if I fought him off, so I tried to do it nicely. A groping sometimes lasted 20 minutes, and in the end Heather and I would stand guard outside the shower and warn each other if he was coming. It became an unwritten house rule between us kids: no girl was to be on her own with Dad. If he called us into a room, we would always take another brother or sister with us.

The gropings happened on a daily basis because he thought fathers and daughters should sleep together. He'd say it was wrong to be a virgin after 16 and we wouldn't be able to have children. He'd use any excuse to do it, saying I would never be able to have a proper relationship with a boy. 'Boys don't do it properly,' he'd say, 'Dads know how to do it right.'

It got much worse when I was 15. We tried to shower when he was out, or go to bed dressed and get undressed after he went to bed. Sometimes he would come in and stare. We were not allowed to have locks on our rooms and he had cut holes in the walls so that he could watch us undress. My old bedroom looks like a sieve.

Another time Dad broke the door in when I slammed it in his face. He was livid and threw the hoover at me for refusing him.

When I wore my school uniform he kept putting his hands up my skirt, so I wore skirts as seldom as possible. I knew it would be tempting fate to wear one, so I used to try to look as much like a boy as I could. He didn't justify what he was doing, he just said I was growing up.

He'd think every woman wanted sex. Once he pinned me to the lounge floor and I was really frightened. I screamed to Mum to get him off, but she said he was only playing. He did this to me and Heather all the time, and he even harassed my friend, grabbing her breasts.

He started touching me up in front of the family, and it got worse and worse. No one ever said anything about it to him, or told him not to. He once put his hands up a friend's skirt when he gave us a lift in his van and we had to climb over the front seats and into the back. He said it was an accident!

When I was well past my fifteenth birthday I was allowed to wear a bra. Mum got me a pink set of underwear and I was so proud of it I got one of my sisters to take a photo of me wearing it. The photos came back and I showed them to Mum. Dad wanted to know what they were and I had to show him. He took two of the photos, one showing me in my underwear and another with me wearing a nightdress. He said he was proud of his daughters' bodies.

We didn't discuss anything with anyone. It was all behind closed doors and I was too scared to tell the teachers.

Heather and I shared a room up until the time she disappeared, and we discussed never letting him go too far. She was affected by this quite badly, more than me. She was so miserable, but she never talked about it. She just became a loner and a bit of a recluse. She wanted to be on her own and do things on her own. Her ambition was to run away and live in the Forest of Dean.

She was fascinated with that area. She liked the outdoors and the feeling of freedom. She was withdrawn and reserved and she never had a boyfriend. She didn't want to do what normal people wanted to do. She wanted to live like a hermit. She never wore shoes—she liked to walk barefoot everywhere.

I think if he tried to rape her she would never give in, and he would have to kill her. I think that's what must have happened.

Dad wanted to know every detail of our periods and at what time of the month they occurred. He'd call it rag week. From the age of 12 he kept in his little black book the dates of all our periods. If we were on he would leave us alone. If he asked I always used to tell him I was on. When it was the 'time' as he called it, we weren't allowed to ride our bikes, play games, run, or go to the fairground. Don't ask me why, it was just one of his stupid ways. It was like being an invalid. He taunted us and told the other kids not to go near us.

Often Mum and Dad used to walk around with no clothes on, no matter who was in the house. Mum never wore underwear and Dad used to grab our hands and put them up Mum's skirt and then push them in our face. 'Smell that, that's your mother', he'd say. She took no notice, even though his hands were often black from work. In the summer she would just wear an apron.

I remember we were not allowed to be on our own with

78

anyone who had left home. Anne-Marie left when she was 16 and when she came back with her husband for a visit I got belted for talking in our bedroom with her on her own. Dad was really paranoid about us talking to outsiders, and I think that was one of the reasons he had all the speakers wired up.

Basically I lived in fear of being raped. I thought it was inevitable. When Mum went out and I was left alone with Dad, he'd get out a porn tape and make me watch it with him. I hated it and was so embarrassed I kept trying to make excuses like getting up to make a cup of tea. That used to make him cross and he'd make me sit down next to him, so I would have to watch it.

Once Dad put a video on for us and it was Mum having sex with a bloke. He turned it off, but he used to sit one of the children down to watch other blue movies. He'd say the little ones used to be glued to it.

When Heather went, Dad touched me more and I felt worse because I didn't have anyone to help me. I don't feel bitter about Stephen not stepping in. I don't think he could have stopped it. Dad would grab me, touch my breasts then take my bra off and fondle me. He was really disgusting. A lot of times he tried to make it look unintentional by sort of brushing past me, and he would say he was only playing. But I knew what he was doing, and I never blamed myself.

He would get nasty and really aggressive if I told him to leave me alone and pushed him away. The best thing was for me to try to find a happy medium, a sort of jokey way of telling him to leave me alone.

If we were playing or laughing he would say we were on heat. He'd shout out to Steve: 'If you want to get Mae's knickers off, get in the bedroom and do it.' Sometimes he would grab us both and pull Heather and me to him. We tried to fight him all the time, but there was no point in screaming.

Because we went through it at the same time Heather and I didn't have to warn each other. We knew when it was coming, and tried to stick by each other. We didn't have to tell each other that Dad was interfering with us because it happened all the time. He'd come into the bedroom first thing in the morning because he knew you probably didn't have much on, and last thing at night. He would just come in and rip the quilts off.

We had two single beds at either end of the room. Once he poured a bowl of water on our heads to make us get up. He thought it was funny. We hadn't woken up quickly enough for him. We wore nighties to bed to try to cover ourselves up, and the whole atmosphere was really making Heather miserable. Dad would come in quickly, pull the quilts back and sometimes get on top of us, go out and then come in again a minute later when we were getting dressed and fumble with us.

The last two or three years Heather was more sullen than usual. She had bitten all her nails, so she couldn't scratch him. She became quite nervous and used to bounce back and forth on a chair repetitively, like a kid.

Stephen ...

Dad used to chase Mae and Heather around and touch them, grab their breasts or grab them between the legs. Mae was so against it she used to scream at him to get off. He would be alright at first, just messing around with her, but when she tried to run he would get aggressive and start calling her a lesbian and stuff. He used to say: 'What sort of girl is it that won't let their dad touch them? Every girl should let their dad touch them.'

I felt angry, really bitter towards him, especially when he used to tell Mum that Mae wouldn't let him touch her. He used to call them bitches and frigid and Mum used to laugh. She never told him to stop doing it.

Mae...

When I was 16 I pretended that I was sleeping with my boyfriend Rob so that Dad knew he couldn't break me in. He used to ask me what it was like with Rob, then he'd ask Rob: 'How was she?' but Rob would never answer; he didn't like that aspect of my dad.

Obviously all this stuff going on at home made me nervous with men. I was okay kissing, but if it was going any further I used to pack them in. I didn't want to go the next step. I was scared and I'd make my excuses, although I knew I would go through with it one day.

My parents were so open about sex, people used to say that it must be great to be able to have boyfriends round to stay. The problem was, we wanted normal family life, we wanted them to say: 'No, you can't have sex before whatever age,' or 'You're not having a boy stay under the same roof.' But my mum and dad would do the opposite and grab them in.

I remember the first time Dad met Rob, and he was soon pushing him into my room and making him stay the night. In fact Rob used to sleep on the couch in my room but Dad thought we had slept together. It suited me because I knew Dad would leave me alone.

When I did start having sex, it seemed dirty to me and it wasn't what I wanted it to be like. Dad would ask Stephen's girlfriends: 'How was it?' And he'd say to Heather, one of my best friends at school who was going out with Stephen: 'If you really want a good time, forget Stephen, have me.' To other girls at school he would say: 'If you want a real man, then I'll do it,' just out of the blue.

Mum said he was very wham bam. He didn't kiss—only once in a blue moon—there was no affection. He wasn't an affectionate person because he was more crude than loving. I got the impression he'd get more fun out of watching and hearing it than ever participating. But if we wouldn't let him touch us or come near us, he accused us of being lesbians and hating men.

He was also fascinated with women's problems. I had thrush once and he made me tell him all about it, all the symptoms and everything. Then he gave me a big lecture on it. Anything I said to Mum would get back to him and he would want to talk you through it and show you pictures.

Another time I had cystitis and I was reading a leaflet on the subject. He completely took it over and he went through it all with me because there was a diagram of a woman's insides. I thought: 'God, that's it then, once he knows something about you he won't leave you alone.'

The result of all this was that by the time I started my first job at 16 I had no confidence whatsoever. I hardly spoke to anyone, and wouldn't have been able to explain how my brothers and sisters were half-caste kids. The truth would have sounded a bit odd.

What was confusing was that Mum was a really nice mum if she wasn't being nasty. And if Dad hadn't been abusing us, he would have been a really good dad. I don't know why they had to be like that. I didn't think there was a way I could get through to them.

I couldn't ask him why he was doing this to us. There was no point appealing to Mum. She knew about it, but she ignored it. She'd just say that Dad was playing, she never really put it down to much. I think she thought that as he wasn't really hurting us, there was nothing to worry about.

I'm going to ask her about it one day, if I get brave, ask her why she ignored it. I really want to know.

Chapter 7
Heather

Heather West was last seen by Stephen and Mae in June, 1987.

Mae...

Sometimes I found it hard to get on with Heather because she was so different. Stephen punched her on the nose just before she left. I think he feels a bit guilty about that now. She didn't cry though—she was hard. She was very similar to Mum, she could be hard towards us.

I remember Heather was really miserable just before she disappeared, because Mum and Dad were nagging her about getting a job. She had been to a party with Anne-Marie's little girl and some of the mothers had complained because Heather had been swearing. She got told off by Mum and Dad, and Heather cut Anna off for telling Mum, saying she was never going to speak to her again. That was the 17th of June, so it wasn't long after that.

The night before she went, she was very upset. She had got a job as a chalet cleaner at a holiday camp in Torquay and was really looking forward to it. But that night, for some reason, the job was cancelled. I don't know why. Heather went to bed sobbing, and cried all the way through the night. I had never seen her like that before. You couldn't have cuddled her, she wasn't that sort of person.

In the morning she was back to her usual self, looking miserable, biting her nails and sitting on the couch bouncing back and forth as she sat. I don't remember the last words I said to her, just how she looked and what she was wearing. She had black trousers on, which were a bit short, and a very vivid pink and white T-shirt with the word 'spike' across it, which she had worn for the school play.

I remember it was raining quite hard that day. Dad had to take the day off because his job was working outside. I don't know exactly what he was doing. Stephen and I left for school at eight in the morning and Mum left to take the younger kids to school at around 8.30.

Most days Mum would be back in the house for about 9.30 and then she would pick up her trolley and go shopping. Heather had left school already and didn't have a job, so she stayed at home.

When we came back from school, which must have been about 5pm, Heather had already gone. Mum was quiet. She and Dad said they wanted a word downstairs and said: 'Oh, your sister has gone'. Dad said to me and Stephen: 'It's just me and you now'.

We know now that Dad had thrown Heather's clothes out for the bin men. Nearly all her stuff had gone, only a few things remained. Dad had packed up her bed and said the job was back on and she had left with a girl in a Mini. As far as we knew, they could easily have rung up and said it was on again. Dad was really calm when he told Stephen and me. I remember Mum standing and him leaning against the bedpost downstairs in the basement. Mum was quite upset. I thought it was because Heather had not said goodbye to her.

The date sticks in my mind because I always remember Dad taking me down to see the basement, which is where we were living, saying we had it all to ourselves now because Heather had left home.

When she disappeared I told the teachers at school she had run away, but they never did anything about it. They used to keep calling me Heather because we were very similar in looks.

Stephen...

I was in the house the first time Heather was supposed to have rung up after she went away. We had three little steps next to the phone leading up to my bedroom, and I was sat on the steps. Mum answered the phone and said: 'Hi, Heather. It's your Mum.' They were talking, and then Mum started to get upset, saying: 'You can't say that about me.' Mum was swearing, and then she said: 'I'll get your father.'

She called Dad, and said: 'She's calling me every name under the bloody sun, you can talk to her.' Dad talked to her, and said: 'You can't say that to your mother, she's brought you up,' and all this. Then Dad put the phone down and said: 'I've calmed her down now. She'll speak to you some other time.'

A few days later it rang again. Dad answered the phone, and said to Heather are you all right and so on. Then Mum spoke to her. Afterwards Mum said Heather had said she'd pop in or she'd write.

We didn't ask to speak to Heather. We knew that wouldn't be allowed anyway. I would wait for them to say: 'Do you want to speak to her?' but they never did.

Knowing what I know now, I think they got somebody to

ring up, so that if we had any suspicions it would calm us down.

Mum did agree afterwards that she took the phone calls. She said as far as she was concerned, it was Heather, and that Dad must have set someone up to pretend to be her, to convince Mum.

Now Mum says that she doesn't know anything about a phone call at all. She says she didn't take the phone call, Dad did.

Mae...

We waited and waited for Heather to write to us, and I wondered for a while if Dad was throwing her letters away. So we kept an eye out for the postman, but still no letters came.

The police told us Heather's body was cut up and put in a cupboard under the basement stairs, and that Dad had done it during the night when we were all asleep so that we didn't hear anything. Apparently it was stored there for a few days. Stephen and I would have slept just a few metres away from her body.

Mum cried a lot when Heather left. We asked Dad why she was crying and he said it was because of Heather. It was an unusual sight to see, because she was usually quite hard. Mum kept wanting to stay in with me and Stephen. She said it was because she knew we were upset. But Dad had said she had to go out, presumably to a client. I don't remember whether she went out or not.

I think we were more shocked than upset. We weren't crying. It was just that Heather hadn't said goodbye. It was a bit odd after that, because the three of us had always been together but now it was just two. Stephen and I got much closer as a result. Heather had been more distant.

After that Mum and Dad were much better parents. Their attitude changed towards us. The abuse from Dad still went on, but they bought us bikes and Mum mellowed out . She wasn't nasty any more. After Heather went, she never hit me again. You could really see the change for the better, and that's why we kept thinking: 'God, if Heather comes back we will tell her that life's good here and that we've been given bikes and things like that'.

I always thought Mum changed because Heather had gone. You know, they had lost one and they had realised they were chasing their kids out by their behaviour. Maybe she thought we were going to leave home, too. I don't know.

I know Anna must have felt guilty about her row with Heather because she went down on the train to Butlins to try to find her at the camp. Of course, she wasn't there and they couldn't tell her anything about Heather.

It was always Dad who'd say he had contact with Heather after she left. He'd say he had seen her on his rounds. Mum never did say that. Mum didn't try to contact her at Butlins because she said Heather would contact us if she wanted to see us. Heather knew where we lived.

Mum never suggested calling her, or going to see her, because her attitude was that Heather was doing her own thing. After the so-called phone call about Mum it was as though Heather hated Mum, so Mum didn't speak about her any more.

After a few years, we got really worried about Heather and me and Stephen filled in a Salvation Army form for missing people. We wrote to Cilla Black at *Surprise Surprise*. That's the TV show where she brings people together who haven't seen each other for years. And we wrote to another TV show called *Missing*, which tries to find missing people. But we didn't get any acknowledgement from either of them.

Then we told Dad that we were going to the police station to report her missing. He sat us down and told us that Heather was involved in credit card fraud and that if we went to the police, we'd be dropping her in it. We sort of believed him, but after a while we stopped believing that he'd seen her; why would she contact him and not us?

Years later Dad changed the story to: 'Did you know your sister was a lesbian. I caught her peeing on the bed'.

Dad built a barbecue opposite where Heather was found. If you were cooking you would be facing where she was buried. We had the old pine table on top of her. It's sickening now that I know Heather was under there. We had birthday meals and things out there, when Mum would cook sausages, bacon and burgers. The younger kids used to love them. Dad would be doing nothing. He didn't participate. He'd just come out when the food was ready.

We used to be out in the garden with the music on and laughing. It was like dancing on her grave. He and Mum used to sit out there for hours after he put the pond in. And he always used to be out there sweeping, going round on his own, as though he was really thinking hard about something. When the patio was down he'd have a sudden burst and go out there sweeping the lot.

I think Dad has mocked her death by telling lies about her. It's one thing to kill someone, that's bad enough, but to tell the lies that he did makes it seem so much worse. He didn't have a good word to say about her even after he had killed her. She had to be a lesbian or a drug dealer, and he used to tell his workmates as well. He could have said something nice, like she's got kids and is really happy. When I start to forgive him I remind myself of what he's done, and then I hate him again.

I heard that he was angry with me when I told the police about him abusing us, after the final investigation began and the police were digging up the garden. But when Heather's body was discovered I didn't want him to get out again, so I told the truth about his abuse of us kids.

I can't forgive him, for as much as it was her, it could have been me. They told me I was close, just because I was a female. I fought him off as much as she did. Mum and Dad always said they loved all their kids the same, but how could he? Heather would have never forgiven him if it had been me. I'm still angry about what happened to her. I keep thinking how scared she must have been in the last two minutes of her life. That upsets me.

Chapter 8
Rape

In August 1992, Fred West was charged with raping a 14-year-old girl. In Britain, there are well-justified restrictions on the reporting of rape charges. These restrictions are particularly severe when the victim is under age. We have no wish in this book to flout the law, but the story that follows cannot be ignored or omitted, because it is pivotal to the uncovering of the full horror of 25 Cromwell Street. When the police realised Fred West was capable of the rape of a minor, and were also told by his daughter Anne-Marie that he had abused her, they began to search much more diligently for the missing Heather. The police believed Heather, too, might have been raped by Fred and could provide important evidence.

Stephen...

I was at work and got a phone call from a CID officer who said they wanted to see me about a serious matter. He told me Dad had been arrested for raping a girl, and Mum had been taken into custody as well. I rang Mae and she picked me up from work and we went home. We weren't too surprised because we knew what he was like.

Mae...

Mum was inside the police station for 24 hours and when she came out she told me to leave the house because the police would want to interview me. I think she thought I might say some bad things about both of them. Very early the next morning the police arrived at our house with social workers to take all our younger brothers and sisters away, to put them into care.

Mum pushed a policewoman down the stairs and they grabbed her and twisted her arm behind her back. She shouted to the kids: 'Don't you dare say anything,' as she was dragged away. She was arrested because she hit a policewoman, and she was charged with neglecting two of her children.

Stephen...

I knew the girl who was supposed to have been raped, so I spoke to her and asked her if it was true, and she said: 'Yes, it is'. I believed her because I knew what Dad was like and how he often threatened to have young girls.

Mae...

I wasn't in the house at the time of the rape, and if I had been I like to think I would have done something about it.

I was told Mum had gone out and left the girl with our brothers and sisters downstairs watching television. Dad came down and asked one of my sisters to make him a cup of tea. He had planned everything so carefully and so wickedly. Then he got the girl he wanted to rape to carry two bottles upstairs to the bar. He followed her upstairs and then locked the door leading to the stairs behind him.

The next thing the kids downstairs heard was her screaming 'No, don't, no'. He used lubricant, but didn't use a condom. One of the older kids told a younger one to knock on the door,

94

which he kept doing. Dad shouted out 'What do you fucking want?' And he replied 'Your tea is ready, Dad'. Finally Dad came down and he shut the door, leaving the girl upstairs.

Dad shouted at the brother who had interrupted him, and my younger sister very bravely asked if she could go upstairs and see the girl, who she realised had been raped. But he said: 'She's busy.' My sister got Dad his cup of tea and then went upstairs anyway. The girl was crying and saying over and over again: 'I hurt, I hurt,' and 'He hurt me'. She told how he had held her round the throat at one stage and how she was really scared. I think he would have killed her if my brothers and sisters hadn't been downstairs.

What really made me cry was that it didn't just happen once, but four times in all. He said he hadn't done it properly and it would cause medical problems if he didn't finish the job.

Afterwards, Dad was in a bad mood for a week. I think he knew he was going to be in trouble, and he was right.

The girl told a friend of hers, who blurted it out to her mother, who called the police. Dad said he was going to kill her. At first the girl said she didn't want Dad punished, but it had gone too far, the police weren't going to let it drop there.

We decided we'd go along with whatever the girl wanted us to do and say. But then I got a very strange phone call from Dad, who said: 'You know what that girl is like at making up stories.' He was trying to convince me I shouldn't believe her. I pretended to go along with him.

I went with Mum to see her solicitor and he read the girl's statement to us. It was awful. I realised what the girl had suffered could easily have happened to me, and I felt that I could almost have signed my own name at the bottom.

When Mum and Dad realised the girl had told a lot of people

what had happened, they called a family meeting and warned us all to keep quiet and say nothing.

Stephen made a statement saying *he* had raped the girl, and not his dad. He was willing to take the rap because he said he was younger and could do more years than his dad could. We went mad when we found out. But the police knew it was all rubbish and they didn't take much notice of it. Stephen, I think, was charged with wasting police time, but nothing happened about that, either.

I had a secret meeting with the girl, who had been taken into care, and she said she didn't want Dad charged. She thought that she would be allowed to go back to her home if the whole thing went away. I was in a similar position so we agreed that, to keep the family together, I'd lie to the police. We thought that if the charges were dropped then all our younger brothers and sisters could come back to Cromwell Street and we'd be a family again.

So in my statement to the police I said my dad was brilliant and nothing like that would ever happen. I knew it was wrong, but it was what the girl wanted. She didn't want to give evidence against Dad, and she wanted her life to return to normal. I couldn't say anything against him myself because I thought—well, he's our dad after all. I was also scared of losing my mum, who was sticking by Dad. It put us all in a very difficult position over loyalties and doing the right thing.

My sister Anne-Marie had made statements to the police against Mum and Dad, saying Dad had abused her. She also backed up the girl's original story that she had been raped. So Anna was effectively kicked out of the family. Mum put the phone down on her whenever she rang up. Anna was a witness for the prosecution so Mum wasn't allowed to speak to her.

One night shortly afterwards, Mum was in a bit of a state and said she wanted to sleep on her own upstairs. At 6am she wandered into the living room as if she was drunk and called out my name. She fell on the settee and was mumbling. I checked the bar to see what she'd drunk but nothing had been touched. I looked by the side of her bed and saw an empty box of Anadin with all the 48 tablets gone.

I called an ambulance and she had her stomach pumped and we waited with her until she was well enough to come home. She looked old and frail and nothing like Mum. It was as if all the energy had drained from her body. We didn't tell Dad what had happened, but he found out later.

The trial lasted about three minutes because the girl refused to give evidence. The three counts of rape and one of buggery were dropped. Dad was really happy to have got off, although he thought in his own sick way that because he had been found not guilty, he had done nothing wrong. He said: 'I'm home for good,' when he saw me back at the house. It was the happiest I had ever seen him. I hugged him although I knew he was guilty. All the charges against Mum were also dropped and we thought it was all over.

We were wrong. The kids stayed in care and 25 Cromwell Street was never the same again. There was no more laughing and playing, and with such a big house, it was cold, silent and empty. Knowing now what happened to Heather and the girl, I'm pleased the kids were taken away, definitely. They are safe, which is very important to them and to me. They are all together and are fed properly and kept warm.

It's a relief that they had time to settle into new homes and lives so that, when the bodies were found, they weren't involved. There's a big age gap between us all so we don't have a great deal in common. We were a close family but if you're brought up by different people you tend to grow apart.

Mum and Dad didn't want to have anything to do with social services when the children were taken away from them. They were offered supervised visits but turned them down because they didn't want the social services there. So, since 1992, they didn't officially see the children at all. They only sent letters or cards on birthdays.

After the kids had gone, Mum got rid of the blue videos, the sex books and anything pornographic like the sex toys and dildos. She said she didn't want them in the house again because it had lost her her children. When Dad was released later in the year he was livid about losing all his stuff. He wanted it all back, the same as normal, as it had been before. He demanded that they start up their porn collection again. He wanted her to go back on the game, but Mum refused to have anything to do with it. She stopped everything completely and never gave in to him again. Even her regular man, the father of two of the younger kids, was banned from coming to the house. Mum even took the video camera back which was on an HP agreement.

There was a lot of tension between them by then and they were not getting on very well, and hardly ever talked. He was away a lot on jobs and she got used to him not being around. And whenever he tried to grind her down about seeing other blokes, she froze him out.

I know that Mum has walked past her kids in the park and had to pretend that she didn't see them, to keep the court order, but they did sneak back to Cromwell Street sometimes to visit.

It was different for the younger kids because the girls were half-caste; Dad wouldn't touch them because of their colour so I think they have better childhood memories that I ever will.

Chapter 9
Clues

In the aftermath of police questioning about the rape, Stephen and Mae began to discuss more sinister possibilities.

Mae...

When Dad was charged with raping the young girl, our half-sister Anne-Marie went to the police and said that Dad had abused her as a child. As a result, they made me go to the police station with them and tried to get me to say that Dad had abused me too. The girl wanted the charges dropped, so I lied to them and said that Dad had never touched me.

To back up Anna's claim, the police wanted to talk to Heather to see if she had been abused by Dad. She had disappeared pretty suddenly, so it looked suspicious to them, bearing in mind the rape allegations. The police obviously thought that Heather had been raped by Dad and that was why she'd left home.

They asked all of us loads of questions about where Heather had gone, if we'd heard from her, and if Dad had been touching her. Stephen and I were questioned for hours. It was the first time we had any real contact with Hazel Savage, the police-woman who was heading the investigation, and she said that she was going to find Heather, no matter what. She said: 'One good thing that's going to come out of this is that I'm going to find your sister.' We didn't like Hazel, but we thought that if she'd find Heather, then that was alright with us.

Stephen...

Some of the police took the attitude that the whole family were scum. We thought they were rude and arrogant. Sometimes they'd just push her way into our house and never wait on the doorstep to ask if Mum was in.

When I was being interviewed by the police about where Heather was, one of the police officers just came in one day and said: 'Face it, Stephen, you're an abuser and you've been abused, so stop messing about'.

We told them what Mum and Dad had told us; that Heather had gone to work in a holiday camp in Devon and that we hadn't heard from her since.

To get more evidence against Dad, the police got a warrant to search 25 Cromwell Street. They had been told by the girl that Dad had videod her rape, and they wanted to find the tape.

The search was really thorough—in the freezer, behind the skirting boards, in the hoover bag, everywhere. Then this policeman said that they had been told to search the house as if they were looking for a body, and started to walk round on the patio outside, checking to see if the slabs had been recently moved. I turned to Mae and said as a joke, but loud enough for the policeman to hear me: 'I suppose they think that Heather's under there now.' After all, they had been questioning us about where she was for days.

Anyway, the police didn't find the video, but they did find

photos of naked children, and home made videos of Mum and Dad having sex. That's why all the younger kids were kept in care.

The police stopped bothering us for a while. They were busy looking for Heather, and life settled down into a routine again.

We would go with Mum to visit Dad in Gloucester prison where he was originally kept on remand on the rape charges, and he started talking really strangely. He was crying and said that he'd done stupid things at night, when we were in bed. He said that he had done the worst crime that we could ever imagine. He became all pathetic and for the first time in our lives said: 'I love you.' It was the first time I had seen him cry. He seemed scared to death.

We started freaking out, wondering what the worst thing he could ever have done was. With Heather missing, we began to wonder what he could mean.

Mae...

When the rape charges were dropped and Dad came home, he promised us that he'd change and that everything would be different. He said that Heather had visited him in Birmingham when he was on bail and that she'd be home within a week. He also said he had seen her at a community centre in Gloucester, but I checked and she was never there. We didn't really believe him, and Mum just told Dad to shut up.

He never mentioned the stuff that he had said in prison again. I think he realised how he had nearly given himself away. We didn't ask. We weren't afraid of him, but we didn't really know how to ask. We didn't want to know.

Stephen...

At night, Mae would come and watch television in my room and we'd talk about Heather and what had been said. We discussed what we'd do if we found out that Mum and Dad had killed her. We used to stay up into the early hours of the morning, whispering about it and asking each other what we'd do if it was true. We thought that Dad might be capable of it, but that's different from really believing that Heather had been murdered. We both said that we'd run like hell and leave them to get on with it. It wasn't as though we really thought they'd done it, but we did wonder where Heather was, and what Dad had done that was so terrible.

Mae...

We started to set traps. It was about this time that *Prime Suspect 2* was on television. It's all about a girl that's found under a patio, and there's a background of pornography and stuff.

Stephen...

The programme was a repeat. We'd watched it before, without Dad knowing, so we knew what was coming. We thought we'd get him to watch it, and see what his reactions would be.

It was in two parts, with the news in between. We knew Dad would be waiting for the news, so that was our excuse. We just put it on.

There was just the four of us, Mae and me, and Mum and Dad. Mum and Dad were sat next to each other on the sofa, and me and Mae were in armchairs on either side of them. We talked to each other across the room, so we were able to see them from the corner of our eye.

Mae...

They watched the television and we watched them like hawks, looking for a flicker of emotion. But there was nothing.

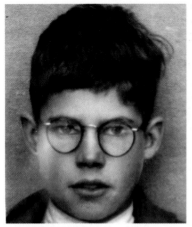
Frederick West, aged about seven

Rosemary West, as a young schoolgirl

Fred and Rose West, shortly after they married.

Above: Rose West's parents
Left: Fred West's parents

Above: Rose West with her mother, Daisy, and one of her brothers
Left: Rose West, right, with Fred, Anne-Marie, Heather and Mae

Fred West, cycling on the hills near Gloucester

Fred and Rose West in playful mood on a seaside holiday. This picture was probably taken at Barry Island

Camping holidays were part of West family life

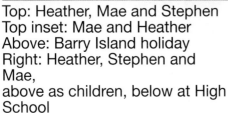

Top: Heather, Mae and Stephen
Top inset: Mae and Heather
Above: Barry Island holiday
Right: Heather, Stephen and Mae,
above as children, below at High School

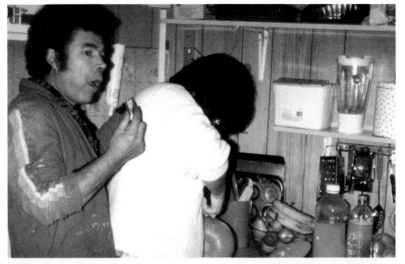

From the family album:
Top: Fred and Rose in kitchen clutter at Cromwell St
Centre, Left: Rose with a neighbour's baby, Right: Rose clowning in Halloween outfit
Bottom: Fred at Cromwell St

"A paradise sort of place"–Rose's lounge, above, with mural (this picture taken after the room had been stripped)
Left: a typical door decoration in Rose's section
Below: Rose in the king-size bed with the lace canopy

More sinister sights. The cellar beams, above, with holes cut to suspend the bodies. The children, who occupied the cellar, used the holes to make swings.

The basement at Cromwell St, with children's drawings on the walls, below. The fresh cement in the centre marks the spot where a body was found.

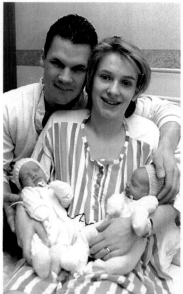

Above: Stephen and Mae outside 25 Cromwell St
Above right: Stephen and his wife Andrea on their wedding day
Below right: Stephen and Andrea with their twins

They didn't react to it at all.

Stephen...

They just looked straight through it. They didn't pass any comment. They were staring at it, studying it. The only other programme they would watch in the intense way they watched that would be the news.

We felt that they would get up and turn it off, but they didn't. Thinking about it, it was pretty unusual to see them sit there and watch the whole thing through. They didn't normally watch programmes like that at all. They would watch comedy, or the news.

Mae and I talked about it afterwards, and said how quiet they were, and how they were staring at it. They went off afterwards and talked to each other, and we wondered what they were talking about, and whether they were talking about the programme.

But we were pretty satisfied then that there was nothing untoward going on. We thought that if there had been, they would have turned it straight off. Now we think maybe that would have been too obvious.

Mae...

The story line in *Brookside* was all about a family killing their sexually abusive father and burying him under the patio, and me and Stephen watched Mum and Dad to see if there was ever any reaction to that. There never was. All we had were suspicions, and nothing conclusive at all.

Still, we were beginning to get worried. We talked about what we were thinking to the other kids. They were still in care, but they used to sneak back to Cromwell Street. Thinking back, there were clues to what was going on. I remember picking up a pot from the lounge and finding the top had been super-glued. I asked Mum what it was but she said it was nothing and looked embarrassed. I kept asking her but she wouldn't say, and then we got the top off. It was filled with ashes, and she told us it was 'burnt knickers'. We pissed ourselves laughing, but she didn't explain. It had been on the sideboard like an ornament for ages.

There was other stuff too. We always thought that Dad was really house-proud because he wouldn't let anyone change anything in the house or the garden. We weren't allowed to bury our family pets in the garden. They said that being children, we'd want to dig them up later. Knowing what was buried under there, it was a good thing none of us disobeyed them.

The house extension that Dad had built was massive and, after all the kids were taken into care, we didn't really need it. I suggested to Dad that we knocked it down and built a car park instead. He was furious and told me that no-one was to touch his house. Anyone digging any foundations would have stumbled across at least one body.

There were other day-to-day things, too. Dad always had loads of purses with money in them that he said he'd found. Looking back, no-one's that lucky. Some of them must have been from the victims. Mum never remarked on these finds, she just accepted the gifts.

Meanwhile, the police search for Heather was carrying on, unknown to us. They couldn't find any record of her going to a doctor, claiming benefit or any National Insurance records. The search was widened and Interpol were contacted to see if she was working or living abroad somewhere. Again nothing was found, no trace of Heather anywhere in the world.

Months later, the kids were talking at their care home about what Stephen and I had said about Heather possibly being murdered by Mum and Dad. A social worker overheard them. The police were called and they took statements from all the kids. On the strength of that, a police warrant to dig up the garden of 25, Cromwell Street was issued. It was February 24th, 1994.

Book II
Police

Chapter 10
Safe Houses

February 24, 1994 had started much the same as any other day at 25 Cromwell Street. Mae had gone to work at an insurance office, and came home at lunchtime to watch Neighbours *with her mother and have a bite to eat.*

Mae ...

There was a big police van on the corner. It wasn't that close to the house and I didn't take much notice of it. We don't live in a good part of town and it wasn't that unusual to see the Old Bill about. As usual the door was open and I walked straight in to find Mum lounging around.

About half-an-hour later the doorbell rang and our dogs started barking. When I opened the door, there were five plainclothes police officers, four men and a woman, standing there. They said they had a warrant to search the premises for the body of Heather West. I was pretty shocked because a body meant that they thought she was dead. But they seemed to be certain about what they were looking for.

They didn't ask if they could come in. They just pushed past the door and asked if my mum was home. They went straight through to her, and without saying a word they served the warrant on her. She read it, handed it back, and then one of them put it on the table in front of her. At first she just said: 'This is stupid,' but then she got more and more abusive. They said they were going to dig up the garden and she got worse and worse. Mum hates the police and went immediately on the defensive with them. But they were serious about what they were doing and she couldn't stop them.

One of the officers, whom we knew, said he was going to dig up the garden. Another said I had to make a statement. All I wanted to do was go back to work, but they said I should stay. By then Stephen had come back home. He was really agitated and said: 'Don't go Mae, don't go with them.' They cornered Stephen off and he kept shouting that I shouldn't go with them to Gloucester Police station.

Stephen ...

I was in town sorting out a few bits and pieces. I had a day off work and was just taking things easy, looking in the shops. As I walked down Cromwell Street there was this white van and a whole load of blokes looking at me. I thought it was a bit strange but I didn't take any notice. I went into our house and saw Mae with Mum sitting down on the settee. There were five CID officers in the room and I must admit I was a bit confused. There was a tense atmosphere and Mum kept saying how stupid it all was.

I asked one of the officers what was going on and he told me they were looking for Heather and thrust a search warrant into my hand. I read it and told them to wait until Dad got home. The officer told me they couldn't wait and they were digging up the garden whether Dad was here or not. I was very angry and demanded to know whether they were going to put everything back. He just said: 'We'll see,' and we started arguing about the patio slabs. During all this my mother was staring at the floor. She seemed really shocked. The only other time I had seen her like that was when Dad was arrested and charged with sex offences.

The police seemed to be trying to separate us and kept asking Mae to go to the station and make a statement. I told Mae not to bother going and not to let them ruin her life. Then I tried to get hold of Dad on the mobile phone but I couldn't get him to answer. Mum was starting to get really upset and rang Dad's boss. She was crying and told him she wanted Fred home straight away. She sobbed" 'I don't care where he is, I want him home now.' Finally we got word to Dad and he left the job he was doing at 1.50pm saying he was on his way home.

I went into the garden and found out that the digging team were planning to wheelbarrow all the earth through the house and out through the front door. I told them that it wasn't on, and suggested the fence could be taken down at the back and they could get what they wanted out that way. All the time I kept telling them the whole thing was stupid and a waste of time. We had been grilled enough when Dad was arrested before and now they were going to put us through it again. I told one of the detectives that they were going to end up making fools of themselves and he just replied: 'That's up to us,' and walked away. I wanted to know the reasons why they thought Heather was buried there but they wouldn't tell me.

Mum was very confused and I went and sat down next to her. It was obvious the police didn't want us to get in their way, and they weren't very pleasant about it. I decided to read the warrant again, but in truth I couldn't understand a word of it. It was all typed on a blue page with different bits

111

filled in. All I can remember was reading 'search for the body of Heather West.' Then they all started coming in with their tools and spades. It sounds a bit odd but we were introduced to the various policeman and they told us what they would be doing and where they were starting.

One policeman was going to sit in the garden all night, on guard as it were. When we were told that no-one could go out of the back door I thought he was joking. It sounded ridiculous, as if they were pulling our legs. Mum burst into tears again. The thing that was puzzling me was Dad, where was he? He should have been home in 20 minutes but it was already nearly 3pm.

Mae...

The policewoman who questioned me, Hazel Savage, seemed to think that Stephen and I were the biggest liars ever and we hadn't been honest with her. She was quite blunt and said that they were looking for Heather's body and they were going to find it. I asked if that meant that she was dead and Hazel said: 'I think you know what I'm on about.' She reminded Stephen and me that we had started the rumour that Heather was in the garden and that we knew all about it. But when Stephen said it to the policeman, it was meant as a joke.

Anyway, she said that Stephen and I must have known all about it but we had been scared too much by our parents to tell anyone.

Stephen...

I kept calling Dad and although the phone was ringing, he didn't answer it. I finally got through to him just after 3pm and he was driving. I said: 'Dad, it's Steve, are you coming home or not?' He said he would be home shortly. I asked him where had he been but he just told me not to worry.

He asked what was going on, and was really calm and polite, which was very unusual for him. He was normally quite aggressive when he spoke. When I told him what was happening he asked how Mum was and said he'd be home soon. Our whole conversation went right through me. It was so strange, he had never talked to me like that before.

Meanwhile all hell had been let loose in the garden as the search team were ripping up the slabs with pick axes and smashing them. It was clear they had no intention of putting them back down again. That's when it started to hit home what they were doing, and what it meant. I realised that this was serious. It was a strange feeling, seeing people digging up your garden to look for your sister's body.

After they had taken up four rows of slabs they started digging with shovels. They were sweating like hell, and then a mini digger was brought in to plough up the garden. Mum remained sitting down and wouldn't look outside—she never once peered outside from the moment they started.

Mae...

We found it fascinating. We wanted to watch. We drew the curtains for Mum so she wouldn't accidentally see anything. She was very upset and kept asking where Dad was because he had been a long time and still wasn't home.

Stephen...

It was now after 5pm and he still hadn't come back. Derek, Dad's boss, said he had been up to the place where Dad had been working and was told that he'd left before 3pm. Dad finally turned up at 5.40pm. He didn't whistle or call out as he usually did, he just strolled in. The police didn't seem anxious to find him or care where he was. They seemed happy he was not in the house getting in their way and causing trouble.

113

Mum had started doing the washing up and he went over to talk to her. They were whispering all time and went upstairs for a bit so that they could talk on their own. I don't know what was said but I went down to the station to make my statement. Hazel Savage asked whether I had been talking to Mae about it because apparently our statements were very similar.

Dad was also at the police station and I caught a glimpse of him staring at the wall in another interview room, and it upset me. He was completely blank, empty, like he was dead—he was just sitting there motionless. He came home about an hour later just after Mum had been interviewed at Cromwell Street, she'd refused to go to the police station..

Mae...

By the evening, it was too dark to carry on digging in the back garden and they asked us to put the floodlights on, saying they would pay for the electricity. When Dad came back they had all gone except this one policemen who was left out there sitting at the bottom of the garden reading a book.

Stephen...

I thought it was hilarious. I looked at him and I thought: 'You poor bugger, its freezing cold.' I asked him if I could let our two collies, Benji and Oscar, out to go to the toilet, but he said no and asked me to go back inside.

Mae...

All Dad was concerned about was getting caught fiddling the electricity meters. God knows why, with all the trouble he was in, but he was trying to work out a way of turning off all the lights quickly and changing the cable over. He couldn't take too long about it because he was worried the policeman in the garden might come in and catch him.

Fiddling the meter was something he had done for years. We had two meters and the faulty one was in the hallway. Two weeks before the meter was due to be read he would route the supply back so that it only showed a minimal usage. We had the heat on all the time and the tumble dryer was in constant use so, over the years, he must have saved thousands of pounds.

We didn't eat that night, but sat drinking lots of tea. We expected Dad to be ranting and raving about what was happening but he didn't. He was strangely quiet, as though there was nothing particularly wrong. He took the dogs for a walk in the park, which was a bit unusual, and then had a shower and sat on the sofa in his underpants watching the news.

We were never allowed to talk to him when he watched the telly so we let him be. We knew when not to ask a stupid question. Perhaps, we thought, everything would be back to normal soon.

He and Mum continued to talk in whispers, so we didn't know what was really going on. I decided to go to work the next day, as normal, but as I went out Dad asked me to look after Mum. I asked him where he was going and he just repeated himself. I didn't understand what he was talking about, and came home from work early because I couldn't stand the tension any longer.

The people at work were understanding. I told them that I had been a witness to a road accident so I had to spend time at the police station, giving a statement. Not everyone believed me.

Stephen...

The next morning the police were back and Dad asked me to clear all the tools out of his van, which was parked outside the house. Dad sat there playing with an old lighter and then said: 'Look, son, look after your Mum and Mae. I'm going away for a bit.' I didn't understand and told him the police had got nothing on him. He said: 'They don't need anything to arrest and charge you,' and got up and walked away.

Derek rang and asked us to move the van away because the press, who were camped outside on the doorstep, had seen the number on the side and had started calling him. Just before I left I saw Dad staring out of the bathroom window, looking out into the garden where the digging had started again. He gave me a look that sent a shiver down my spine. His eyes bore straight through me. It definitely wasn't normal.

When I came back Andrea, my girlfriend, told me that Dad had been taken to the police station again. Mum was in the front room crying her eyes out saying: 'I don't know what's going on, I don't know what's happening.' She said Dad had told her to keep out of the way and that the police wanted to speak to her mum.

Mum said: 'I don't want them to speak to Nan. I'll kill that bitch Hazel Savage if she ever speaks to my mum. Nan is ill and I don't want her to be involved.' I made Mum a cup of tea and Andrea and I sat talking to her until two CID officers came in, saying they were arresting her for Heather's murder. Mum, who had stood up said: 'What?' and fell back onto the settee, crying.

I started crying, and she went upstairs to get dressed. When she came down again, Mum took her cigarettes and lighter and went out the door without looking at me or saying goodbye. I rang Mae and she came home immediately.
Mae...

At that point, I told my boss the truth about what was going on at home. He could hardly believe his ears, but he did say that I could take time off and that he would keep my job open. At that point I was still hoping that things could get back to normal, but things got worse at work. A day later the press started phoning up all the time, and they had to open a special phone-line for them. I realised that I could never go back there. *Stephen...*

We refused to believe that Mum and Dad wouldn't be coming home shortly. We still didn't take it seriously. As we were not allowed in the garden, we watched from the windows, sitting on stools eating crisps and drinking tea.

Then one of the police found a small bone. It was only about three inches long and it was clearly not human, but they were making a big fuss and came to look at it. It turned out to be a chicken bone. I started making clucking noises in the kitchen and jumping about. Mae did the same, and we thought it was a great laugh.

We didn't realise what was about to unfold. With Mum and Dad at the station, the police were more sympathetic to us and that night Hazel rang saying that Dad's solicitor Howard Ogden wanted to speak to us. A copper called Bob, who had been friendly towards us, gave us a lift and we walked into Gloucester police station. It was the pink interview room where we had been so many times before.

Howard walked in with Dad's voluntary helper Janet Leach and said out of the blue: 'I'm sorry to tell you this, but your dad has admitted to the killing of Heather.' We couldn't believe it. I slipped down the wall and sat on the floor crying. It was such a shock, and we were not prepared for it.

Mae...

We asked how he did it, and Howard said she had been stran-gled. I found it hard to accept, and didn't break down at all. We said that he'd only admitted it because he was under a lot of pressure and he must have made it up. It sounds strange, but at this point I was annoyed with Steve because he was cuddling his girlfriend and I had no-one. I felt all alone. But then we were told that as we stood there Dad had been brought back to the house and was pointing out where she was buried. I told Howard that Dad must be sick and that he needed help.

Stephen...

They had marked the spot where Dad said she was buried, and they dug until quite late under a huge floodlight. Mae and I couldn't sleep that night and we stayed in the same room together. It wasn't until the following evening they found something. Apparently Dad had said that when they got down so far there would be a stream running through the ground. That hit home. We thought: how does he know this?

Mae...

There was a huge canopy over the excavation, and it was awful waiting for something to happen. We closed all the cur-tains at the front because the press were trying to take pic-tures of us. Bob eventually came in and said they had found two leg bones. It had taken so long because they had dug the wrong way, across the legs.

Stephen...

We asked if she was whole, and Bob replied: 'You wouldn't have wanted to see her.' Later, he told us the bones had been sawn in half, but when they put them together the ends fitted. It was the worst time of my life. I had convinced myself that they would not find anything.

The police called the pathologist, and he confirmed everything. Then, while he was there, they showed him another bone and he told them it was a woman's femur. That was all they needed to know. They started digging all over the place.

They had to pump out the rain from the trenches they had dug, but they worked until they got the whole of Heather's skeleton. It was only then that it really began to sink in what was happening. The police didn't say it was Heather, but just said that it was the body of a young girl.

Then something absolutely horrific happened. The tarpaulin was unhooked, and it blew up as Mae and I looked out of the window through the rain. There was a huge hole about six feet deep, with all the clay piled up on the side. Beside the earth were these little pieces of bone lying on the ground. I expect they were bits they had sifted out.

Mae was appalled and said she felt sick, and turned away. I was really shaken. It was the worst sight I could ever have imagined. Things were getting worse all the time. First Dad, then Mum, now Heather. I thought at first it was going to be Heather full stop. However they confronted Dad about the other bone, which was found in a different part of the garden, and he agreed to be taken back to the house.

Mae...

Neighbours and friends from work dropped in, crying and saying that they didn't believe Dad could have done anything wrong. One lady from my work came round and told me that God would protect me and that He was watching over us. At that time most people were pretty supportive.

We didn't want to leave Cromwell Street in the first place, but Superintendent Bennett insisted, because he said they were going to have to take over the whole house. We were worried about what was going to happen, and who would look after our dogs. They were eventually taken to the RSPCA.

Stephen and I said that we were not going without Mum, who was being questioned. We distrusted the police, but I must admit these ones did seem different. They treated us well, more like victims, really. They used to come in and explain what was happening, and what they were going to do.

Anyway, they finally released Mum on police bail one night at about 8pm. When she came in she looked a bit of a mess. She was very quiet and she just sat down. Then she said: 'I'm spending one night here and then we are off, and we're never coming back to Cromwell Street again.'

We didn't argue. That night we all slept in one room, Mum and I on a mattress on the floor, Stephen and Andrea in the double bed, and the cat and the two dogs were also in the room. We wanted to be together and Mum didn't want to be on her own, which we could understand.

By this time we couldn't see out into the garden because the police had taped black bags to the French doors and bathroom windows. It was horrible. All we could hear was the digging, and the sound of policemen chattering.

The next morning the police took a long time to come back, but when they did we said that we wanted to move. The police took Mum and me to see the safe-house, and then there was a delay while they got the electricity and gas turned on.

The house was in Longlevens, Gloucester and looked nice from the outside. But there were no carpets or curtains inside, which made it seem very bare. We were only allowed to pack up essentials because the police said everything else was 'evidential', and might be needed for court. When we packed up what little we were taking, a policeman said he had to search it all, so we had to stand there while this PC went through all our bags and underwear and everything. Even he got bored in the end and skipped over a few bags which were then chucked in a van along with the television, video and everything.

The safe-house was a smart, three-bedroom place, but we all used to congregate in the same room downstairs because there wasn't much furniture. Steve put up curtains where it mattered, and Mum and I tried to make the lounge look reasonable.

However the pressure started getting to me and Stephen, and we started fighting. He hit me after my cat walked over the puzzle he was doing on the table. We hadn't even been rowing or anything, it was as crazy as that. He lashed out at the cat first and I was livid. Bagheera was very special to me. I named him after the Jungle Book character.

I hit Stephen, first punching him in the kidneys because I was angry, but I didn't hit him that hard. The next thing I knew I was on the floor. I wasn't out cold but I didn't feel well for a couple of days after. Mum was furious with him, saying: 'This isn't what we need right now. We should be sticking together.' She even rang the police and said she would rather be locked up if her son was going to act like his father.

The row had been heard by the neighbours, who called the police. But when they saw it was us, they didn't intervene. Mum told Clive Stephens, the detective who was looking after us, and he warned Stephen that he should be supporting his family, not hitting me.

I love Stephen and I think he was genuinely sorry afterwards, but it did really hurt me that he had done it at all. He kept saying he didn't mean it , and since then he has never laid a finger on me.

121

Mum didn't want to be alone and we kept her company all the time. We just watched loads of videos, did puzzles and talked. It was claustrophobic. Mum and I shared a bedroom, but she used to get up around 6am. She once had a cleaning job, and was just used to getting up at that time.

We didn't have a washing machine, so she used to do everything by hand. Then she would watch TV. The first couple of weeks we were on the phone constantly, because that seemed the only way to communicate with the outside world. The bill must have been enormous.

We were just talking to friends and family about the situation. It was interesting to found out who your real friends were, and who was trying to sell stories about us to the papers.

Stephen and I did the shopping because Mum was worried she would be recognised, and we heard that there were reporters looking for us. Mum used to cry a lot, but on her own, not in front of us.

We talked constantly about Dad. It was difficult to take it all in. The newspapers were full of it, and we bought stacks every day and we watched every news bulletin on all the channels. The police used to come round at 11am and brief us on any updates about the search at the house. Mum used to do the cooking and we bought food from the money we had from Dad's last wage packet.

I can't describe the feelings we had when we were watching the news, we were all sort of numb. We hated the police coming round. We always felt shocked, and sat quietly after they left. It was all so hard to believe.

At night Mum would sleep with me, and sometimes in the

night I would wake up and hear her crying. Then she used to sort of rock herself to sleep again, like she did with us when we were babies.

We tried getting into some sort of routine and if Stephen went out I would stay with Mum because we didn't want to leave her on her own in case she tried to take an overdose.

After Stephen talked to the *News of the World,* the police moved Mum and I to another safe house behind Dursley police station in Stroud, and for weeks we didn't tell Stephen where we had gone. He was sending flowers to Mum through the police, but she didn't want him back. Mum was furious, not because of what he had said particularly, though she was hurt. It was the way he had done it. He didn't tell us what he was up to, and he should have.

It was miserable there. We had no heating and no cooker. We were cold and hungry. The house really was a dump. It had dead flies on the window sills, stone floors, and smelt of damp. But we were not there for very long—only about a week—because *Today* newspaper got a picture of Mum out shopping and followed us back to the safe house.

This time we were moved to Hales Close in Cheltenham, and the house was much more modern. It was a proper police house for families in the force. But the woman next door was a bit abusive, endlessly trying to find out who we were.

Mum and I used to play scrabble and Mum would always win. The rest of the time we used to listen to tapes, watch telly and talk. Mum read nearly every newspaper every day. She didn't care what people were thinking about her, but used to point out the bits that were wrong in the stories. She never showed her emotions much anyway.

She knew she had been a prostitute, and the papers were full of stories about her and Dad. But a lot of them had been exaggerated. Eventually, it all got a bit too much and she stopped watching the telly and reading the papers. But I kept them all and cut out all the articles about the family.

Mum knew she was going to face the same charges as Dad. He was being charged with new murders almost daily. I think she was sort of waiting for it, knowing it was inevitable. She said if she ever did time and was sent to prison, she was always going to say she was innocent, right to the end.

A week before Mum had to answer her bail, it was around April 18 1994, there was a knock on the door and two officers stood there and asked to see Mum. They told her she was being arrested for the rape of a young girl and indecent assault on a young boy. She quietly got dressed while I ran upstairs and sat in a bedroom. I didn't want her to go. Clive Stephens told me that Mum was also probably going to be charged with murder, and I might not see her again.

I rang Stephen and told him what had happened, and we sort of made it up. Then he and Andrea came to stay with me. But when Mum appeared in court, the address was read out and everyone knew who we were.

Through the night there was a 24 hours police presence and I started to feel uneasy. The next day I was sitting on the porch with Andrea because it was hot, and a little girl rode past on her bicycle. Then her Mum came after her and grabbed her, leading her away in tears saying: 'I told you not to go near those people.'

It wasn't long before Stephen blew his top again. He was then living with his girlfriend Andrea and her parents in Brockworth, but he was still pretty stressed out. One day he reversed over his tool box in the van and went mad, throwing them all over the road. There was a big row, and he stormed out.

Not long after that, he had a big row with Andrea and grabbed her by the throat one night. I think he grabbed her after he'd found out that she'd gone to the phone box on her own—he didn't like it. Stephen had moved back in with me at the safe house at that time, and he told Andrea to get out. When she started packing he grabbed her back and said: 'You're not leaving me.'

The following day she found out she was pregnant and told him. He hit her again, over something else, something stupid. She had a black eye after that ,and told everyone she had banged it on the sink when she was cleaning her teeth. But when I got back from a trip a light socket had been smashed. I knew Stephen had been in another rage. Andrea told me he had swung a punch at her, she had ducked and he had hit the two way switch instead. Enough was enough.

Andrea and I decided to pack everything up and go back to Brockworth together. We were absolutely terrified. She wasn't meant to tell me, but she then confessed that Stephen had hit her, which I already knew. We locked all the doors and windows and waited for him. Sure enough he rang up blaming me for everything and saying he was going to kill us both. After that call we rang the police and a WPC came over and when Stephen turned up she said to us: 'Lock me outside.' She was only little and was very brave, stepping out to meet Stephen, who was waving his arms in the air and swearing. The policewoman told him if he didn't calm down she would arrest him. He calmed down a bit and a few hours later Andrea went back to him and I stayed with Andrea's parents.

125

My position was made clear to me after Mum's arrest; the police didn't need to provide accommodation for me and they gave me seven days notice to get out. I registered myself as homeless with the housing people in Gloucester, and Andrea's mum and dad put me up for a few weeks.

I got very depressed because Mum wasn't with me and I just didn't know what to do any more. Mum was being held in cells at Cheltenham police station and I did all her dirty laundry for her, although I wasn't able to see her. With every bag of laundry she used to hide a letter, and I used to sit in the car park of the police station crying and reading it.

The police finally allowed me to visit, but told me we were not allowed to touch each other. I had just had my 22nd birthday and Mum had made me a card. I went to show her my new watch, but my arm was grabbed by a policeman as I held it out to her.

During this time Stephen and I were continually going backwards and forwards to Gloucester police station, making statements. Then Mum was transferred to Pucklechurch Remand Centre, where I visited her twice a week and brought in clothes and cigarettes for her. She was watched 24 hours a day and had two guards with her when she went to the toilet.

Most of the time she was in her cell, keeping herself occupied by sewing, embroidery, crochet and writing letters. Her bed was skinny and very hard with no springs. She had a window with bars on, no carpet and a little tin bin and a square table. A lot of the inmates screamed abuse when she walked past but a few of them befriended her and slipped letters under the door.

Some of the police officers who dealt with her in Cheltenham still write to her.

Chapter 11
Confession

After the bodies had been discovered, Fred West con-
fessed to all the crimes with which he had been charged.
Stephen was allowed to visit his father on a regular
basis whilst Fred was held at Gloucester Police Station.

Stephen...

My mind couldn't take everything in at first. I just
didn't want to believe what people were saying
about my dad. The police asked me if we ever saw
Dad digging in the garden or the basement, and I remembered, when I was a five-year-old kid, watching my dad do
all this work around the house.

When we were very small, he made us a concrete paddling
pool just outside the bathroom window. I could picture myself watching Dad in his dirty overalls, digging this massive
hole, bricking round the edges and cementing the bottom. We
didn't have the pool for long—he filled it in after a while.

The police dug it up, and I must admit I was quite interested
to see our old pool. Then they broke the bottom. We were
watching the garden when they did this, but didn't see anything because they kept canopies over everything. I was told
there was a girl under there. We had been paddling in this

pool, which he had put in basically to concrete over this girl.

Quite early on in the investigation I heard that he had cut them all up and sawn their heads off. But I needed to hear him say what he'd done himself. Until I did, all I knew was what other people had been saying. To be real, I had to hear it all first hand.

I saw him when he appeared in court. I was sitting there with my girlfriend, and didn't feel too bad. He came up the stairs from beneath the court, and I felt sick and went cold. He looked withdrawn and had lost a lot of weight. He didn't see me.

I wasn't crying or anything. All the reporters were staring at me and making me feel uncomfortable. I was staring at Dad when they read out the charges, and they said: 'Do you understand the charges?' and he said: 'Yes.' That was it, I was crying then. I couldn't believe that he understood what they had just said to him. The body count was eight by then. For him to say yes, he understood he was being tried for murder, made it hit home that he might have actually done it.

He still hadn't seen me. They told him he was being remanded in custody and he was taken down the stairs. I lifted my head up as he went out of view, and then at last he saw me. He put his head back and his hand up, and I winked at him, then he carried on walking down the stairs.

When I first visited him, the police said I'd have to be searched. They searched me everywhere. They said it was just routine, but I was surprised.

I was really nervous. I was going to run out because I didn't think I could look him in the eye. They warned me that he was upset and told me to be careful, and then there he was, just sitting there, when I walked into one of the interview

128

rooms. He got up, put his arms around me and hugged me. I said: 'Alright, Dad?' He replied 'I knew you wouldn't let me down.'

He didn't stop holding my hands all the way through, both of them in his. That was the first time he had ever held me like that. He said: 'I'm sorry, son.' I couldn't cry. I was very shocked, and I felt very hard, cold. He asked: 'How's your mum? I'm sorry I've done this to all of you. You'll understand it when it all comes out. When I tell the truth, you'll understand.'

The second time I went to see him, I wasn't searched. I wondered why. Dad told me he had asked for me to be searched because he didn't know how I was going to react. He said: 'I was scared. I'm sorry, I thought you'd have a go at me.' I told him I was hurt by him saying that. I know people would say: 'I'd sort him out with a machete,' or something like that, but I know they'd have felt sorry for the bloke. I felt so sorry that he could mess his life up, and everybody else's.

I didn't hold back. I said to him straight out: 'You either did it or you didn't,' and he replied: 'I only made love to them when I thought they were dead.' God help us all, I said to myself.

For some reason, he wanted me to know the full truth. The half-truth was shocking enough, but he said: 'When they start telling you that snuff movies are involved, don't believe them. It was not quite like that.' I thought to myself—fine—he's got that one off his chest.

He never really told me why he did it, what drove him. But he said: 'I've done it all.' I visited him twice for half-an-hour at the beginning of all this and I believe that what he told me then is the truth.

I said to him: 'Were they cut up?' and he said: 'You'll find out in time.' I said: 'This is what they are saying, Dad, that you cut these people up. Why?' He said: 'Well, I used my brain.'

I asked his solicitor, Howard Ogden, why he'd cut them up. 'Is he sick or was it deliberate?' Howard said to me: 'You think about it. He's quite good with his hands, and he's got this problem with this big body and he has to put it into a hole. The best way for him to do it is to dig a small hole, which is quicker, cut the body up, and chuck all the pieces into a small hole. He used his brain.'

Dad was really distressed when he talked to me in the beginning. It was not really a time for questions. It was quite clear that he had done it. He just wanted to tell me in his own way, in dribs and drabs, and without hurting me.

The fact is that he never wanted any of these women to go. That's reflected by them being buried under his feet in the back garden. I think he wanted complete control. He wanted to map out their lives. Heather wanted to go and that's why, I think, he killed her as well, his own daughter.

He thought to himself—I can put them down there and they won't be away from me. He put the ones in Midland Road where he was living, then he put the other ones in a field as near to his house as he could get away with. The Fence, where his first wife Rena was found, was where he used to make love to her and sit laughing and joking.

He said to me: 'Can you remember helping me dig holes in the basement when you were a kid? We dug holes in different places in the basement.' I said I couldn't remember, but he said: 'We did it together, you know.' Then he said: 'That's where the girls were found, in the exact holes.' It drives me crazy when I think about it. It's like some TV horror film which has come to life.

I can't believe Dad made me dig my sister Heather's grave. I was asked to dig a pond in the back garden during half term. He told me: 'I want a hole there, about four feet deep and six feet across, and I want you to lay blue plastic in the hole and leave it.' Then one day when I came home from school it was filled in. He said he had changed his mind about the pond and wanted one at the bottom of the garden instead.

It really upset me, once I realised I had dug the grave for Heather. I think it's really sick that he could ask his own kid to do something like that.

The way things look, I think it may have happened at around 9am, after we had gone to school. Dad said it was early morning. He strangled her in the hallway. He got one of the black bins from the house, cut her legs and arms off, put her in the dustbin, put the lid on and put her in the cupboard under the basement stairs. Then, he said, we went to bed at 9pm, and he buried her in the garden.

It's so weird—I wanted to hate him when he told me that. Then I think: he is my dad and I still love him. And you see his face and you feel sorry for him. Then I think of Heather and I hate him again. At the time, I felt different every day. I used to wake up in the morning and it was a task to get through the day. It was a battle with whatever you were going to be told next. Every day was like I'd just been told.

Dad said all the police kept questioning him about was how he tortured them. They had their nails pulled out and their fingers cut off while they were hanging up, and cigarettes stubbed out on them. The only thing that was done outside Cromwell Street was when they were cut up. A story in the press said he mutilated the bodies in the bath, but Dad never said that. Apparently he used a butcher's knife. I've never seen it.

He didn't say why they were tortured, but they were. He slept with them after they had died. I think he was saying that he killed them in the house, then took then away to cut them up and brought them back to the house. He sexually assaulted them in the house, then he tied them up and tortured them, then he killed them, then he did whatever he did to them.

The victims were found in bits. They were found with their legs on top of their heads and bodies. The heads were all cut off and put in plastic bags. Basically they had been cut in half. It was only the heads that were in plastic bags. Rope was found with the bodies as well. Then he put them in the van and took them out at night, chopped them up, brought them back in these tubs and buried them.

I couldn't picture which tubs he was talking about, but I spoke to Mae one night and it clicked. Dad told me about some bins he used to put the bodies in. They had holes drilled in the top in three corners and he had made lids for them and put padlocks on them. He said it was to let the smell out.

There were two of them. I remember we used to play with them as kids, and made them into wendy houses. I think they may have been fibre glass. The tubs were around a lot. They were three foot long, two foot high and two foot wide. We used to put sheep dung in them and use it as manure for the garden. Dad never put the manure under the trees and we had lots of it. In the summer the smell used to come into kitchen— it was awful, attracting flies and wasps. We never saw it being dug into the garden. It was never used.

One bin disappeared, I think, but with the other one I remember we went out on a Sunday to collect sheep manure to make the trees grow. This was a family day out and we had a bag each and a little spade. We had to shovel it in and carry it home. It was fermenting for about seven years and it stank. I don't remember him ever bringing those tubs into the house. The police think it was done outside, there was no way he could have done it in the house.

He admitted everything at first, but changed his mind as soon as he went into prison and said: 'You know I haven't done it.' He blamed everyone but the milkman. I knew he was talking a load of rubbish and that he did it all. I don't think he wanted me to hate him for all that he had done. He could see I was distancing myself from him.

Near the end, he was still sticking to the story that someone else had done it, but said he'd had a little part to do with it. The truth was mixed with so many lies. He said he had stabbed Annie McFall in the caravan site at Brockworth because he loved her and couldn't have her, or something. He used to tell me a machete was found buried with one of the bodies. He asked me if I knew where it had come from. The next time I saw him I mentioned I had seen the brother of one of the victims, Mary Bastholm, on the TV. I said: 'You don't know anything about it do you?' And he looked to the ground. I said they were going to go into the café and knock this wall down which he had built. He said: 'It's a waste of time looking in there.' I went really cold. I didn't know what he meant. I said: 'Why's that?' and then Dad said he didn't know anything.

We carried on talking and he said they are just going to have to carry on finding the rest out themselves. 'I'm fed up with helping them,' he kept saying, 'I'll be out of here in 12 years and we'll all go back to live again in Cromwell Street. If they find any more bodies I'll never get out. Why should I help them? What are they going to do for me?' Dad stopped co-operating with the detectives because if he told them every-thing, he would have had no control. They needed him and he knew it.

The police did not give him one ounce of space. They were bombarding him with questions, and he didn't know what to think. He was so glad at first to get it off his chest, but once he was in his cell at Winson Green he thought to himself: 'I've helped them and now I'm stuck in here so I'll tell them noth-ing more.' He did break down during the questioning, and he had a doctor with him who gave him some tablets. He went into really graphic detail, saying what he had done with the bodies.

I can't get it out my mind, what he was describing about events in the basement at home. He wasn't making much sense. My understanding of it was that the holes in the beams in the ceiling were big enough to get hands and wrists through. All he would do was make two nooses round the legs and pull them up through the holes. That would allow him to muck around with them when the bodies were upside down. He only did things to them when they were dead. I can hear us laughing and joking in the cellar, but my mind turns to the horrific things now. To think we were playing on a swing, hanging there on the beams—innocently—that makes me think. That was our home as kids, we used to sleep in that room on and off throughout our lives. My sisters Mae and Heather and I, were chucked down there a lot because we were not really allowed upstairs.

We put thick nylon rope up and used the beams in the ceiling as a swing. We used to hang about from there. Dad said to me: 'I hung them from the beams. It wasn't when they were alive. I cut their legs off to get them in a bin. Then I'd take them out afterwards to do something to them.'

It was hard to understand what he was saying. He was blurting it out and not talking in sentences. Dad used to sit down there for ages, having a cigarette and a cup of tea and talking to us all. It was really good, but to think what he knew, it's sick. I suppose he thought it was nice and close to those girls.

I don't want to think about what went on down there with Dad and his victims, it's too horrible. He was trying to tell me the truth, but he didn't want me to be shocked by it. He even became a third person describing someone else as the murderer, saying he had to protect him. I think one day I'm going to be so pissed off with him for screwing up my mind by telling me what he did and destroying my feelings for him as a real father.

He'd say: 'Don't you know whoever killed them took them away in black dustbins to a farmhouse. They were put in a vehicle.' But half way through his story he kept saying: 'And then I did this and I did that.' He said it was at this farmhouse, they were taken there to be cut up and tortured and whatever and to be brought back from there to be put in the garden at home.

I asked: 'Where is it, where is it?' He didn't tell me at first, but several visits later said: 'I know where it is. I followed someone there once. It must have been this person all along.' I asked again: 'Where is it?' He said it was towards Berkeley power station. I decided on my way home to have a look and sure enough it was there. I was so shocked I didn't think about it again. I just tried to ignore it.

The farmhouse is about 25 minutes drive away from our house. I wasn't expecting anything at all. I drove up to it and my legs were shaking and my heart was really jumping about. I was so horrified that I drove off as fast as I could.

At the end of the day, I wish he hadn't had told me anything. But if there was one thing about him, you couldn't stop him talking. I just feel he wanted to tell someone. He wanted someone to know before anyone else did. He wanted to tell them because then he could keep the upper hand on everyone. He just had to get it out really.

He looked really pale and thin when I saw him next. He wasn't crying, but he was chain smoking. The window was open, and it looked into the street. We met in an old interview room with white steel and wooden walls full of small holes. There was a speaker for interviews and a tape recorder on the table. Dad was smoking like a chimney, first a cigarette, then his solicitor Ogden gave him a packet of tobacco and he rolled his own. He kept having to ask for a light. All his fingers were yellow because he'd been smoking so much.

He was really creepy at times. I'd try to break the ice and say something funny and he'd look at me stone cold. Then I'd say something serious and he'd start laughing and fall off his chair he was laughing so much. I looked at him thinking, help, I want to go home. I thought to myself—this man is gone in the head.

Ogden and the police were talking loudly to each other, so we could say anything to each other. I said to Dad: 'Look, have they found everyone now?' This is before they found Charmaine. He said: 'Yes, they've found everyone now, but it could change at any minute' I said: 'So they haven't,' and he just repeated himself.

He then said: 'I wanted to see you in here, because they are going to have your mum, and they aren't going to let her back out. They are trying to get things against her. You've got to swear to me now you'll tell her not to come to the police station when she's due back in. Tell her to get out the country, go anywhere.' I told Mae to pass on the message, because Mum wasn't speaking to me at the time.

Then he said to me: 'I can have a cigarette when I want to. They take me out into this alleyway and give me a cigarette. They leave me out there on my own. They let me have a cigarette and then they come round and pull me in. I was looking the other day at the barbed wire. You can come over there and get me out.' And I went: 'Yeah.' He said: 'You could cut that and I'd be away,' and he laughed. I couldn't believe it, he wanted me to break him out. I was waiting for him to tell me the time and what I'd need to carry it out. I knew from the way he was looking at me that he was serious.

I walked down the stairs with him and he was really jumbled in what he was saying. He cried a couple of times when he talked about all the work he'd done on the house, which was now going to be knocked down. He seemed really upset, but only about the house. He then asked if Mae and I were going back to live in Cromwell Street. 'No Dad,' I said, 'I just couldn't sleep at night,' and he said: 'Oh, but it's clean isn't it?' Clean? It's the cleanest house in the street, there's nothing in it, I thought to myself. I said: 'Shut up, Dad, you're making it worse.' He said he didn't want Mum to knock the house down. 'We're going to have to sell it now, aren't we?' he said and I replied: 'Yeah, I'm afraid so.' Then I said that Mum wanted to knock it down, and he went on and on about how it had to be kept standing, like a monument to what he'd

137

done. His house was his life, he just worshipped the place.

He talked about all the work he had carried out and how they were going to knock the house down. He said: 'You've got to get the goldfish out of the house,' as if it was the most important thing in the world.

He cuddled me and said: 'I love you a lot, son,' and he nearly killed me he squeezed me so hard. He said: 'See me as soon as you can. You know if you were in trouble I would be there for you,' and I thought yes, that's true, because when I've been in the shit, he's been there for me. He said he wanted me to keep going to see him so we could both help each other.

He said how easy life was inside the police station and how during breaks in his interviews he was allowed to watch videos. He said: 'It's like a palace downstairs, I've got three cells all to myself, and two more if I need them. I'm cut off from the rest of the prisoners. I have a woman who helps me and gets me fresh fruit and proper meals.' He was boasting how easy life was, to convince himself everything was alright. He said: 'Look after yourself, make the best of your life,' then he put his arms around me and cuddled me and whispered in my ear: 'Tell your Mum I love her—and I'm sorry.' As I was leaving he winked at me. That was the hardest part, walking away. I wanted to stay and sit with him, help him through it.

After his initial confessions Dad started making things up. There are things that will never be known. There are more bodies, but no-one will ever know where. I think if Dad hadn't committed suicide and he'd been sent to prison, he would have confessed to more murders, saying there's one here and one there. He would have played cat and mouse with the authorities, but he couldn't last that long. I think he knew his fate.

Confession

After his series of confessions to Stephen, Fred then started planning Heather's funeral, telling Stephen that she should be buried in the family grave next to his own mum and dad in his home village of Much Marcle, Hereford.

Stephen...

I couldn't believe Dad could say such a thing, having admitted what he had done. There was no way he was going to have anything to do with Heather's burial. It's not decent, it's sick he could think of such a thing. He had done terrible things at night when we were in bed. He told Mae once: 'My life begins when you are in bed.'

When I went to the opening of the inquests, it was terrible. There were the families of five of the victims there and I had made up my mind to go. But it was very hard when I walked into the waiting room. It all went quiet and everyone looked at me. I felt low, embarrassed, and wanted to run out. At the same time I wanted to show my face. I had nothing to hide and I was in the same boat as everyone else. They had all lost somebody and I was a victim as much as they were.

Then Belinda, one of Juanita Mott's sisters, came over to me and asked if I was alright. She started crying because she didn't know what to say to me. It was very awkward. Her mum was terribly upset and being there made me feel sick.

It was heart-breaking when Heather's dental records were read out. I could visualise the teeth they were talking about because her front ones stuck out a bit. She was meant to wear a brace, but she never had one. Afterwards Belinda came up to me, gave me a kiss and shook my hand. Then the other sister came up and said: 'Don't blame yourself.' Then the mum came up and she was really crying, so I gave her a kiss and I think I mumbled: 'It will be alright.' It meant so much to me—it meant they didn't all hate me and blame me for what had happened. I respected them so much for that, because I knew what they were going through.

Chapter 12
Suicide

Stephen...

The second time I went to see Dad in prison he told me bluntly: 'If they take their eyes off me, I'll be gone.' I told him he shouldn't do anything like that but every time I went in to see him he used to cry for the first 20 minutes. It was always on my mind. He said: 'Sometimes the pressure in here gets to you.'

Dad told me if he didn't do it, someone in there was going to. He said: 'See me as much as you can, because I may not always be in here.' He was in tears, crying his eyes out. He said he lived in fear. He really meant that. He said: 'I know everyone hates me in here.' He said the other prisoners shouted and swore at him and called him names. It was amazing that he could turn round and tell me that he was scared.

I don't think he would have told me if someone had had a go at him. He would have said he had sorted them out. He was quite tough when it came to us kids and the odd bloke in the street, but it's different when you are in there. You are pushed down a peg or two. You start to look small with so many other people.

We used to meet in a little private room. There would always be three prison warders present, although they gave us some privacy and couldn't hear what was being said. He always cuddled me when I went in, and when I left. He was determined to keep out of trouble and he called everybody Sir. Even the other prisoners when he saw them. I was with him one day when another bloke came by. He was in there for murdering his whole family and Dad said: 'Hello, Sir.' The bloke just nodded. And he always called the screws Sir. He was always really polite.

When he didn't call me before Christmas, I realised he must be a bit down. I thought I should try to see him. I wrote him a letter but it's still at home on the side. I forgot to send it. I was just waiting for him to call. And when he didn't, I thought he would call in the New Year.

I was going to tell him that this year would be better for him and just see if I could get him through it. When I look back I think he just wanted to see his grandchildren born into the world and then get out. Even if I had spoken to him he wouldn't have told me what he was doing.

He talked about it on a regular basis. He knew he was never going to get out of there. He said: 'You've got to face the truth son, I may be in here the rest of my life.' But I think I would have sensed it if I had seen him. I knew the risk was there. Even when he was held in the prison cells at Gloucester at the beginning, he said he wouldn't hesitate if it got too tough. I told him he had to think of us before he did anything because he was not just killing himself it was us as well. He was crying so much at the time. But after visits he looked better, even though he still sobbed.

I don't think he could accept that life as it was at Cromwell Street was over. At Christmas it obviously all built up. I suppose he didn't owe me anything, but he did owe it to me to not give up. One of the detectives told me that they had evidence that the suicide had been planned for a few weeks.

He always impressed upon me that once I started something I should stick with it. I put a lot of effort into standing by him while he was inside. I tried to write to him as much as I could, at least once a month. And I spent money on tobacco, books and batteries. Every time I went to see him I tried to keep his spirits up. Every time he was low I tried to give him positive things to think about—even if I had to lie to him. I did it just to see if I could make him smile.

Sometimes we used to have a laugh. Thinking about the past and what we had done together made him smile. We talked about the clowning about we used to do, and the jobs we used to go on. The way he used to drive, he used to scare me to death. He was a maniac. I had to have a handle so I could secure myself to the side of the van. I used to hold onto it for grim death.

I blame myself. I feel partly responsible. I can't not. He would have been so desperately upset because I didn't call my son after him. I thought about it for a long time, but decided it would only cause trouble if I did. I know he would have wanted me to carry his name on. I knew it would have made him happy if I had named my son after him. I was the only person he could trust.

Ever since I was young I wanted to call my own child after my mum and now I have. Despite all the circumstances, I don't see why I shouldn't. Andrea and I both agreed it would be nice. I know she was very pleased about it.

My mum will always be my mum whatever happens, but I

didn't feel I could so easily do it on my dad's side. I feel his death has something to do with me. No matter how I look at it, he must have been so upset.

I thought about carrying on the name but I decided not to, because I didn't think it would be practical. He knew I supported him 100 percent but he must have stopped believing in me.

We expected him to call me at Christmas, but he didn't. I heard some people at the prison claiming he was feeling down because we hadn't spoken to each other. I don't know whether this is true, but it sounds very likely. It was definitely in his mind.

I have accepted it now. But there's so much I didn't say. It's the kids which I regret mostly. I wanted him to see them, his grandchildren. In a way I feel quite cross and angry at what he has done. It was very selfish. When I looked at him lying there on a table at the coroner's court, I said a prayer in my mind. I just said how much I cared for him and how much I wanted to stick by him. He seemed so tense. When I looked at his face I could almost see the stress he had been under.

He didn't die a happy man, that is for certain. I just wish he had admitted it and apologised to all the families. I would have found it better and easier to cope with if he had done that before he had gone.

Mae...

I was driving to meet a friend in Oxford when I got bored with the tapes I was playing and turned on the radio. I heard the name Fred West and thought it was just something about the case. Then they said he was found dead in his cell this morning. I thought I had misheard it, but it was repeated again.

I can't describe how I felt. I was crying, crying so hard. Luckily I saw a layby close by and pulled in immediately. I sat there in a daze, hoping I hadn't heard the news correctly. I went completely white and was shaking. I shouted out 'No, Dad, why?' I cried uncontrollably for half-an-hour. Anyone driving by must have thought I was nuts.

I started feeling sick. I thought I was perhaps over-reacting, and that it was a New Year's day hoax. But when I saw my friend he asked me: 'Have you heard the news?' and I knew it was true. I always knew he would kill himself in jail. He was terrified, and forever watching his back in case someone had a go at him.

Once another prisoner, serving tea, threw a whole jug of boiling hot water at him. But he ducked and it missed him. After that he was really frightened and was always looking over his shoulder. He would never be able to stand the thought of getting hurt and not being with Mum. I didn't think, however, he would have the guts to do it. They are saying that Dad wasn't that popular inside prison. He was always going to take his life.

I decided not to go and see his body. When Stephen did, he was devastated and it really hit him hard. I know I would have felt terribly guilty if I had gone so I have tried to distance myself from it.

Dad had Stephen and Anne-Marie for support, so I sided with Mum. It wasn't easy, because over the last two years from 1992 I had become close to him again, after he stopped abusing me. I left home at sixteen because he was forever touching me up, but I later returned to Cromwell Street when Mum pleaded with me to come home after Dad was arrested for abuse.

I found he had changed. He began treating me like a real

person. He brushed up past me a couple of times as though he was thinking of trying it, on but nothing more than that. He went no further.

It's quite strange really, but I haven't held that period against him. It wasn't his fault. Sexually, he was weird. That's what I think drove him to murder.

I do forget the bad things that have happened to me. I just forgave him. Despite everything I still loved him. People may not understand that, but he was my dad and I will miss him very much.

I had planned to visit him in jail after his case had finished, whatever Mum thought. I expected him to be found guilty, but it was once he was put away for life I thought I could risk upsetting my mum and seeing him. I know Stephen used to tell Dad: 'Mae sends her love.' I never used to tell him to, but now I'm glad that he did. It helps with the guilt.

In my mind I remember him when he was laughing and cracking jokes. But I don't think I'll ever escape this family name. I believe God has split us up and is trying to kill us all. If it's a nightmare then please God let me wake up now. I sometimes don't think this is happening to me or my family. It feels so strange. I'm waiting for the next tragedy to race round the corner and hit us.

I keep dreaming at night about my dad and see his face rushing towards me. It flashes up to me, coming towards me very quickly, and then goes through me.

I tried to hate him, but I don't think I can. It's as if we can never escape the past. Our destiny is always to be haunted by tragedy and death. It seems like a curse has been put on the family which will never be lifted.

My dad's van which Stephen uses for his work was dying

during the week, and blew up on his death. The battery stopped when Stephen found out about Dad and it just conked out. My car also refused to start which was strange because I'd never had any problems with it before. My cat who I love to bits has been constantly sick and won't eat anything. I was making plans for the New Year and was confident about the future. On New Year's eve someone said to me: 'It should be a good year for you. You look tense. You have to liven up.' The next day I found out Dad had committed suicide. How's that for a good start to '95?

I can't get away from my family name. People have threatened to beat me up if I turn up at certain places in Gloucester. And some blokes who find out who I am just want to go to bed with me to add a notch to their bedpost. When I was out at a club recently, a woman started telling everyone who I was and they all started staring at me as if I was to blame.

Things have never been normal in our family. Every time I think: 'That's it, that's the end of it now,' something else comes along and hits us like a runaway train. I don't know what normal is any more. I reckon normal would bore me. Life after this is going to seem pretty dull when everything has settled down.

Book III
Trial

Trial

DAY 1—October 3:

The trial of Rosemary West opened at Winchester Crown Court to headlines heralding it as "the trial of the century".

Newspaper, magazine and television representatives from the United States, Australia, Brazil, Germany, France, Ireland, Belgium, Norway, Switzerland and Spain joined with colleagues from Britain in the queue for seats in the court.

The presiding judge was Mr Justice Mantell. The prosecution was led by Mr Brian Leveson QC, the defence by Mr Richard Ferguson QC. Newspapers speculated that the legal bills for the trial could run to £1 million. This was on top of the £1.5 million cost of the police investigation, which involved weeks of digging at four sites, including 25 Cromwell Street, and the use of high-tech devices to detect bodies.

The town of Winchester braced itself for a media invasion. Pubs stockpiled beer and spirits. Every hotel room in the town had been booked months in advance. Locals rented out flats and spare bedrooms. The Chamber of Commerce estimated that the city's economy would receive a £500,000 boost. Other estimates put the figure as high as £1 million.

The city had seen celebrated trials before. In 1603 Sir Walter

151

Raleigh was tried there for treason against King James I, found guilty, and sentenced to death. The scaffold had been erected on Castle Green, but Sir Walter was given a last-minute reprieve.

More recently, the court hosted trials of IRA terrorists and other high-profile defendants.

Rosemary West's counsel came to the court with an established reputation for mounting successful defences in highly-publicised cases. Richard Ferguson had helped to overturn the judgement against the Birmingham Six, freed after the court found they had wrongfully been convicted of an IRA pub bombing.

The prosecuting counsel, Brian Leveson, had also been involved in celebrated cases, including the prosecution of the comedian Ken Dodd on charges of tax evasion.

Jury selection took only eight minutes. The first 12 jurors called from a panel of 30 were sworn in without challenge. When the jurors were being sworn in, the judge warned them that the trial would last five to eight weeks.

The jurors, eight men and four women, were then told by the judge they must banish "all preconceptions, prejudice and sentiment" from their minds.

Mr Justice Mantell continued: "Enter upon your heavy responsibility in a clear-cut way, unaffected by anything you may have read about this case, which certainly has its sensational aspects. This is a case which has received a certain amount of publicity and it is going to receive more.

"You try this case, nobody else does. It is your job to try it according to the evidence you hear in this courtroom."

Stephen and Mae did not go to Winchester. Mae was on standby as a witness for the defence, and was therefore excluded

*from the court. Stephen was not called. They stayed at home
in Gloucester, in separate houses.*

  *Mae was by now seven months pregnant, and was sharing a
house with a young sister. Stephen was working as a builder
for his father's old boss Derek, and living nearby. They followed the trial by watching television and reading the newspapers. However Mae spoke often to her mother, and to her
mother's solicitor Leo Goatley.*

Mae ...
I feel really tense. Mum rang before she got ready to go to
court. She seemed alright. We talked for about ten minutes,
but I didn't want to say too much in case I upset her. She
appeared quite calm, although her lawyer, Leo Goatley, is
really nervous. He's been preparing for the case for so long
now. He's lived and breathed the case. He's optimistic, and
is convinced she's not guilty. He wants the best for Mum,
which pleases me. But when you're facing ten murder
charges you can't really expect to walk free.

  I don't know what to do with myself. I'm all over the
place. I can't switch off. The trial will be all over the TV,
radio, newspapers and billboards. I will watch the news to
see Mum and see what clothes she's wearing. I bought them
all for her. There's an emerald-coloured dress, and a black
dress and black jacket, which I ordered from a catalogue.
Mum has lucky charms which she is taking to the court in
Winchester. She's wearing a silver cross. She'll need all the
luck she can get because a lot of people are gunning for her.
Stephen ...
I'm not as close to Mum as Mae, but she's my mother and I
can't abandon her or pretend she doesn't exist. It's not easy,

because she's a hard woman and it's difficult to know what makes her tick. But whatever I think about her and what she's done I still recognise what she's going through in court.

DAYS 2 and 3—October 4 and 5:

Although the trial began officially on October 3, a Tuesday, the jury did not begin to hear evidence until October 6, a Friday.

The intervening days were taken up with legal arguments, conducted in the absence of the jury. The judge ruled that there should be no reporting of these arguments.

Mae ...

In some ways it's a relief that at last the waiting is over, but the pressure I know will build up. I hope I can cope—I hope Mum will cope. I know most people think she's guilty, but I do honestly believe she's innocent. OK, she's done some bad things, but that doesn't make her a murderer.

DAY 4—October 6:

The prosecution outlined its case to the jury, giving its version of how the ten victims met their deaths. "Their last moments on earth were the object of the sexual depravity of Rose West ... then they were snuffed out," said prosecutor Brian Leveson.

Mae...

Despite what the world is hearing about Mum she does have friends. There are girlfriends she's made in Durham prison who send her nice letters. The prison officers at

Durham jail, where Mum stayed before the trial, think she's coming back there. One of mum's friends wrote and told her that they've made up a cell for her. Mum told me: "It's a cheek they're convinced I'm going back there."

Mum's still pretty confident. She thinks she can walk away from all this and start a new life somewhere. Mum wouldn't run away, she said to me: "I'll just say I'm innocent—and that will be that." I don't think Mum realises just what the outside world thinks about her. What really hurts is when Mum starts to talk about being found guilty and how she'd cut us all off—and she would as well.

DAY 5—October 9

*R*osemary West's mother Daisy Letts and sister Glenys *Tyler both gave evidence for the prosecution, recalling the disappearance of Rosemary West's step-daughter Charmaine.*

A neighbour from Midlands Road, Shirley Giles told how Rosemary West had said "bloody good riddance" when relating how Charmaine had gone to live with her natural mother Rena.

Mae ...

I'm getting a bit paranoid about everything. It's getting to me. The prosecution case is really having a go at Mum. Witness after witness is making her out to be evil beyond belief. She was bad, but she says she's no killer and I believe her—I've got to.

Being pregnant is making things doubly difficult. I know weight is hard to lose when you've had a baby, so I'll have to look after myself.

155

It's hard to know what to do with myself. I've started reading books about serial killers—God know why, but I suppose it helps me to think other families have been through the same thing.

DAY 6—October 10

A neighbour, Mrs Agius, testified that Fred West had told her how he and Rose would cruise the streets in their car looking for young girls to pick up. Mrs Agius said that Fred preferred to have Rose with him in the car because the girls would think it was safe to get in.

Caroline Owens, a former nanny, told of the night the Wests picked her up when she was hitchhiking. They took her back to Cromwell Street where she was sexually assaulted by both Fred and Rose and was raped by Fred. Held prisoner overnight, Fred threatened, within Rose's hearing, that if she didn't cooperate, she would be kept in the cellar and 'used by his black friends and when he finished with me they would bury me under the paving stones of Gloucester'.

Mae ...

It's still difficult. Mum is up there in the dock charged with ten murders. I can accept what Dad did—he was an evil monster and nothing about him surprises me. But Mum— well, that's different. I can't accept she would ever murder. I know I'm going to collapse when it's all over, whatever the verdict. We're going, myself and Stephen, at the end of the trial. I know I've coped well without Mum being around, but I don't know how I could manage thinking she was going to be in jail for the rest of her life. I know Mum will never accept being in prison. She will kill herself—and has said so. The thought of her being unhappy makes me unhappy. I know people will say how stupid I am to stand by my Mum, but she's all I've got. Mum herself is finding it tough. She said to me: "I just want it over."

Mum has now completely disassociated herself from my father. She calls him Fred West. Mum says she's finding so much about him from statements made by witnesses. She says of Dad: "He's an animal."

Mum's solicitor Leo has broken many things about Dad which she didn't know about. At times she has to go to the toilet to get a breather because she says it's such a shock.

I'm going to see Mum in Winchester jail tomorrow. I'm nervous about seeing her and hearing first-hand how things are going. She's become institutionalised inside prison and very much used to the life. She doesn't fight the system.

DAY 7—October 11

T*he court heard how the mother of victim Lynda Gough went in search for her missing daughter. Mrs Gough's enquiries led her to 25 Cromwell Street and she re-called that the woman who answered the door there was wearing Lynda's slippers and another item of her clothing. The dark-haired woman was Rose West, said Mrs Gough.*
Mae ...

I've seen Mum and feel much better for it, although she seems even harder than she was before she went inside prison. There's something about her which is so uncompromising.

I was glad I saw her though. Mum seemed really strong.

It's as if she can take anything that's thrown at her. It's scary, really. We do have a rapport, although Mum is very demanding. I spend about £300 a month on her, which puts a great demand on my income. There's a lot to buy, women's things, clothes, visiting her. I don't mind.

  Mum is on a 24 hour lock-up where she is continually watched at all times. She's shattered after a full day in court and can only manage a bit of reading and sewing. She sees her solicitor Leo at the end of the day and then wants to sleep. She says she gets very mentally tired.

Stephen ...

I'm working hard at the moment doing construction work, which means I can, at times, stop thinking about the trial. I don't know when its all going to stop. The stories the witnesses are telling are very frightening and revealing horrors we wouldn't have thought possible. I've got a lot on my mind at the moment. I'm patching things up with my wife Andrea after we had a bust up and split.

DAY 8—October 12

The court heard a succession of poignant statements from families and friends of the victims, giving details of their last known hours.

Then lodgers at 25 Cromwell Street told their stories. Two male lodgers had regular sex sessions with Rosemary. Another told of walking into a room unexpectedly and finding two semi-naked women there, one of them Rose West. The overall impression was of a household where free-wheeling sex was the norm.

Stephen...

I'm following the trial, watching the news and reading the papers. I try not to let it get to me, but you just can't ignore it.

I'm working with Derek, my Dad's old boss, doing all kinds of construction work. I tried working on my own, but it was a lot of hassle.

DAY 9—October 13

Lodgers' accounts of life at 25 Cromwell Street continued. Gillian Britt told how she heard late-night shrieks and wails coming from Rose West's special bedroom. Jane Bayle said that Shirley Robinson, one of the victims, claimed to have shared a bed with Fred and Rose.

Stephen .....

I'm trying to keep my life together at the moment, while coping with the trial. I've been done for careless driving, fined £300 and given six points on my licence. I told them I'd had it rough because of everything and they accepted that. I could have been banned, which would really have screwed up my building work.

Mae ...

Mum's alright. She gave me a call. It's funny hearing her voice over the telephone. She sends me one letter a week these days. The letters used to be a lot longer, but Mum only has the time, and I suppose the energy, to write a few lines saying how much she loves me and everything. I get a bit upset because everyone hates her inside prison. The guards are really offish with her, but Mum manages. She's tough beyond belief. Nothing will break her.

DAY 10—October 16

Miss A, a key witness for the prosecution, took the stand. (Miss A is not connected with Girl A, Rosemary West's daughter.) She described how she had arrived at 25 Cromwell Street and been taken to the front bedroom, to find Fred West there, wearing shorts. Two naked teenage girls were also in the room. One of the girls was tied down on the bed then assaulted by Rose with a vibrator, before being forced to have intercourse with Fred West. Then Rose West had undressed Miss A, who thought: "God, I'm next." Miss A was bound with tape, and Fred West had intercourse with her.

Under cross-examination by Richard Ferguson, Rosemary West's defence counsel, Miss A acknowledged that she had been admitted to hospital with severe depression, and had ECT treatment. She also admitted she had been "seeing things" and had suffered flashbacks.

Mae ...
I'm still trying to come to terms with reading about my sister Heather's murder. I didn't know the details of what happened to her—and I can't really cope with thinking about her final moments. It does horrify me to think what became of Heather and those poor girls. Their final moments must have been agony. It's incredibly sad. God knows what their families must be feeling. At times I feel it would have been easier to run away from everything and leave my Mum behind and start a new life. But I can't desert her. I hope people realise my predicament.

Stephen ...

Like Mae, I've thought a great deal of what became of the
victims. I listened to Dad's confession of what he did. It
was so mechanical, so monstrous, that maybe I couldn't
take it in. Hearing about the bodies and the dismemberment
reminds me of what actually went on. It does my head in.

DAY 12—October 18

T*he day before, the court had heard from Kathryn
Halliday, a lesbian neighbour of Fred and Rose West,
who described daily sex with Rose and three-in-a-bed
sessions with Fred and Rose. However, she said, some months
after the relationship began, the Wests became increasingly
violent and she ended her visits. "I realised I was getting
way out of my depth," she explained.*

*On day 12 Anne Marie West took the stand. She told how, at
the age of eight, Rose West had led her to the cellar at 25
Cromwell Street, then pinned her down while her father had
intercourse with her. She had been bound and gagged because she struggled and screamed. In the ensuing years, she
said, her father had sex with her repeatedly.*

Mae ...

Hearing about Anne-Marie's evidence is really hard. I'm
torn really. I don't really get on with her. We're very different people and she hates Mum with a vengeance. I think it's
because Mum isn't her real mum, though I accept completely she had a very, very rough time as a child. We all
did in our own ways. Yet, I suppose we've taken sides.
Anne-Marie against Mum and me.

Stephen ....

I'm making plans for a Hallowe'en party. I've got to try and live life normally, whatever normal means. I'm trying to get myself together. I'm seeing psychiatrists to try to control my temper and understand what I'm all about. I'm not a bad person, it's just that things happen to me. I need to get myself on the straight and narrow.

DAY 13—October 19

The jury had asked for an opportunity to see 25 Cromwell Street. On day 13 they were taken there by bus, flanked by police outriders, after being warned by the judge that they must not talk among themselves about what they were seeing. They were not to ask questions of the escorting police officers. They must simply observe silently.

The house was screened off to prevent press and television pictures of the jury or of the interior of the house.

Mae ...

I've been watching the news and it doesn't look good. Everybody seems so shocked by what is coming out in the trial. I know it's awful. There's been evidence which has really hurt me. Mum had admitted she did things to Caroline Owens—"I was a bit over the top," she said.

DAY 17—October 25

The final week of the prosecution case was largely taken up with forensic and police evidence. Pathologists described the state in which the bodies were found, including the position of gagging tape and other binding.

Under cross-examination by Richard Ferguson for the de-

fence, Superintendent Bennett, the police officer in charge of the investigation, admitted that the "safe houses" occupied by Stephen, Mae and Rose West for six weeks after Fred West's arrest, had been bugged. Police had been able to listen to every word of conversation in the houses, and at no time had Rose West said anything to indicate her implication in any of the ten murders.

The prosecution concluded its case on Wednesday, October 25. The judge ordered two rest days, Thursday and Friday. The case for the defence would begin on Monday, October 30.

Mae...

I can't give evidence to support Mum and I'm devastated. Mum's lawyer has read a proof of our book and he says there are details about what Mum did to us which could really hurt Mum's case. I've been in tears since being told and feel I've let Mum down very badly. I feel incredibly guilty. I'm meant to be supporting her, yet I won't be called as a defence witness. Giving evidence on my Mum's behalf was going to be very important to her. I'm the only member of the family who's stood by Mum. She was counting on me and I don't know how she's going to take the news that I'm not going to say nice things about her in court. No one is going to say anything good about her.

I don't want to be caught lying in the witness stand. That wouldn't do me or Mum any good. There are things they could ask me which would make Mum look really bad. I don't want to talk about them in court because they'll make Mum out to be a psychopath.

If Mum goes down then I'm going to feel really guilty.

I think Mum has forgotten the beatings she gave me as a child and how she treated us. She would deny it ever happened in court, I know she would.

I've made so many plans for the future and feel my life has been on hold since the bodies were found. It's the waiting, the endless waiting, which gets me down.

I've been truthful in the book and there are incidents which happened I've told no one else. If I thought Mum was a murderer then I'd have nothing to do with her. I certainly don't think she's an angel. Neither is she whiter than white. She was hard when we were young, but I've got to believe she's innocent. I don't think I could live otherwise.

Just because Mum is weird and into kinky sex doesn't make her a criminal.

REST DAY—October 29
Mae...
Leo Goatley, Mum's solicitor, gave Mum the first 160 pages of our book to read, because he said it was relevant. She won't admit a page of it is true, because we have hurt her so much. I was hoping she would never read it, or at least not until the dust had settled on the case. The timing is lousy. She is just about to give evidence and she's read everything I've said about her. She was very offish with me when I went to visit her in Winchester today.

I don't know why Leo gave it to her. I would like to have talked him out of it. He just rang up and said he had given it to her, like it was nothing. He said he wanted to explain why I couldn't give evidence but he could have told her without showing her the whole book. She's had it for four days. Now she feels totally let down because none of us have stood up there for her.

I kept thinking to myself: have I made anything up or got something wrong. But I haven't. All I have said is the truth.

She doesn't see it like that, though. In our family it's an unwritten rule that you shut your gob and the only way you show you love someone is to let things lay and not tell the police or anybody.

There's a gap there now I will never be able to patch up with her.

I've cried a lot over this but now I think: fuck it—I should never have been put in this position. If she was more of an angel, she wouldn't be facing all this. But she isn't whiter than white.

Leo said it would help Mum's situation and that he would get a feel of what Cromwell Street was like if he saw the book. But he never said anything about showing it to Mum.

My visit lasted two hours and it was the hardest time Mum and I have ever spent together. Usually we talk endlessly about everything, but she was much harder and just said she was on her own. She seemed to have lost a bit of hope. She didn't seem bothered either way what happened. She said she's now got complications if she came out or stayed in jail. She won't face the truth. She never has.

For all those years she's saying that she never knew that I had one complaint. Now, suddenly she's facing the lot, having read it all in the book, and she can't take it all in.

I feel like a complete liar, and I'm not. Perhaps I should not have said all these things, but what did she think I was going to write a book about then?

DAY 18—October 30

The defence began its case dramatically by calling Rose West as its first witness. She told the jury of her hard early life, including the time she was abandoned by her mother, and of being raped twice before she was 16. Openly sobbing, she denied ever meeting five of the girls whose bodies were found buried in the cellar and said she could not remember much about the assault on prosecution witness Caroline Owens back in the 1970s.

Mae...

She's honest about that. She's got a terrible memory, it's like a sieve—she can't even remember what she did last week. She said to me: if I can't remember, that's what I will have to tell them.

I think in the 70s she just did as she was told. She was only 16 and Dad stopped her going out and that. If she made him a cup of tea he would throw it at her. He was a right bastard.

Mum did tell us when we were kids that she had been raped. When we got to adolescence she'd say never go in strange cars, and she told us that story about the bloke who raped her. She said if you are ever in that situation, being raped or he might kill you, then give in.

I didn't know about the other rape.

DAY 21—November 2

A succession of defence witnesses told how they had been approached or assaulted in the Gloucester area by a man acting alone, and that they now recognised that man as Frederick West.

Trial

Meanwhile, the defence had asked Barbara Letts, Rosemary West's sister-in-law, to be ready give evidence on Rose's behalf. Mae agreed to accompany her aunt to court, Mae's first visit there since the trial began.

Mae ...

I don't think Mum's case is going very well. Lots of witnesses were sent home despite having sat there all day. Barbara was told that she had put a certain thing in her statement and they weren't sure whether she should take the stand. In the end, she didn't give evidence.

I said to Leo: if you are trying to find somebody who would not say anything against Mum it's going to be difficult. Everyone has got bad points, it's got to come out. No one is going to say she's an angel of mercy are they?

I was surprised the court was so small. I went into the public gallery and had a tour around, but not when the case was going on. I had to sit with my auntie in the witness room. I had a pass to go in, but if I had then I couldn't be with the witnesses, so I decided to stay with her.

I was up at 5am and got there at 9.30am. It was a really long day. I don't know if I will go again. Obviously I wasn't allowed to see Mum. It felt strange to be that close without seeing her. She knew I was there because Leo had told her.

I've been reading everything about the case and have even found out things I never knew. Like, she signed herself out of hospital when she had me and got on a bus against medical advice. She wanted to get home because she suspected Dad was in bed with someone else.

Her version of how she knew about us lot saying that

167

Heather was under the patio was wrong. She said that Steve
went to Anna's and it was shouted out that Heather was
under the patio. It wasn't like that. It had nothing to do with
Anna, it was just us spreading the rumour around, really.

At the end of our last meeting with Mum, when she had a
real go, I asked did she want me to come in again and she
did say yes. Maybe she will have calmed down a bit by
then. I'm getting nervous now because there is probably
only about a week to go.

Stephen ...

I don't know why the defence are calling all these witnesses telling how Dad attacked them. They're just using
Dad as a defence for Mum. That bit about Mum taking
Anne Marie out for drinks when she was 12, and to meet
blokes—that's terrible. I didn't like hearing that. It's going
against Mum when you hear those things.

I am confused, upset about the things I'm finding out
about Mum. We lived a life and Mum said totally the opposite. If somebody took her name off the paper I'd think it
was someone else. There are things told us, and things she's
told the court, which don't match up.

I said to Mae: don't you back down, it's the truth. The
truth always hurts, doesn't it. It's the one thing you can't
face.

We argued about what Mum was saying about Dad. I don't
think anyone's defence should be based on someone who is
dead. Mum chooses to forget things.

I didn't know so much hurtful stuff about Mum would
come out during the trial. It's not nice to hear these things.
Mae says: "I know what Mum's like," but Mae forgives

168

Mum because she needs her support. I don't. Mum knows I don't feel that close to her and I'm not going to hide the fact. Mae and I have had a lot of fall-outs over what we think of Mum, but what I can't do is ignore what I know to be true.

I'll be really glad when the trial is over because it's a strain having your whole world controlled by these other forces. I just want to live my own life with my wife and children. I'd love to escape somewhere like Australia where no one would know me. That's my ambition and dream.

DAY 22—November 3

A hushed court heard tape recordings of Fred West's confession to murdering 11 girls and young women. On the tape he stressed that he had acted entirely alone. "Rose knew nothing at all," he said.

Meanwhile, away from the court, Stephen decided to carry out his father's wish and scatter his ashes. Wanting to avoid cameras and publicity, he set off from Gloucester with Anne Marie and a younger sister in the early hours of the morning, taking the urn containing the ashes.

Stephen ...
Anna is nuts, she's flaming bananas. She knew what she was doing. She just wanted Dad. She rang me, begging me, pleading to me, if she could just hold Dad's ashes. I said: "No, 'cos I don't trust you to give them back." I said: "Dad's wishes were to have his ashes scattered over his Mum's and Dad's grave. Let's go and do it and get it over with. Then we will both know where Dad is." So I picked Anne Marie up and we drove off to the cemetery in Much

169

Marcle. It's pitch black, no lights or anything. I can't find the cemetery, and Anna is saying: "Keep going, keep going," then she says "Stop here". So I pull over and she jumps out of the car.

Suddenly I looked in the back of the car and saw the ashes had gone. She runs across the grass verge and into this house, which I realised belonged to Dad's brother Dougie. I started shouting, and we had an argument. We waited about 20 minutes until Anne Marie came out and started screaming and crying.

Then she goes running across the fields in the pitch black. We're trying to find her and can't. The police turn up and they get this helicopter with heat seeking equipment and dogs.

The police found Anna and then got the ashes back from inside the house. I put them in the boot of the car and for some reason Anna started kicking the car and bashing on the windows saying: "I want to see Dad." I said: "He's in the car. You get in the car and I'll take you home." She said: "I want to see him" and I said: "He's in the boot." I opened the boot and said: "There he is," and suddenly she grabbed him and goes legging it down the road.

We waited an hour-and-a-half, it was 4.30am, and I rang the police who said the ashes were with her and nobody knows who they belong to. I said I could prove they belong to me. I am going to report they've been stolen out the back of my car. Anne Marie said she wanted to pour Dad's ashes into the same pot as his victims, Rena and Charmaine. I can't believe she'd want to mix the ashes of the man who killed his wife and child.

Dad wanted to be scattered there and she's caused all these

170

problems. She said she's got this little room in the house with a low wattage bulb and she's got the ashes in a corner with other memorabilia.

It broke my flaming heart. I just wanted to put Dad where he wanted to go. It's unbelievable. She's got no respect.

Mae ...

I've had a bust up with Stephen. We don't think the same and I get really angry when he goes on about Mum. We fight all the time over this. I am sorry what happened over Dad's ashes. Stephen was heartbroken. He tries to do things for the best but they don't work out. It's not his fault.

REST DAY—November 6
Mae ...

I'm doing the filming for the BBC documentary *Inside 25 Cromwell St* tomorrow. I'm a bit nervous about it all.

Tomorrow the prosecution will be answering the evidence from Dad's tapes, and that's it. The trial's almost over.

Mum's happy with me. I saw her Sunday and she's fine. She's not forgotten about the book, though.

She says about the verdict: "It's 50/50." At the moment she's up because Dad is saying on the tapes that it's him. But she's worried about the prosecution tapes. She told me: "As long as there is a bit of doubt they've got to acquit me."

She has told us what we've all got to do for the verdict. She doesn't want me there. She said medically I shouldn't be there. I'm happy I'm not going. I wouldn't mind if I knew Mum was going to get out, but if she didn't I couldn't take it. I don't want to break down in front of people so I'd rather stay at home. She's asked the nun who befriended her to sit with me when the verdict is announced. I'm not sure what to do really. I don't want to upset Mum.

When Mum talks about being acquitted, she says: "How can I ever get on with my life knowing Stephen'll be telling people what I'm doing." Then she said: "We are going to fall out over this," because she knows how much I think of Stephen.

Mum loves us, which she makes obvious, but she's as tough as old boots. We have these strict rules with her and you are either for her or you're nothing.

She said to me: "If you're mixed up with the f****** press I'm leaving you behind." Mum told me to do the book, and then she has a go at me. Mum has a fairy tale idea of what it's going to be like. She can't walk into a dole office and say—give me housing benefit. She's Rose West, for God's sake. I'm going to wait until she gets out and talk to her.

I have picked up the pieces of everyone in my family's life and haven't had time to get on with my own.

Mum holds my hand all the time when I'm talking to her. I can't just abandon her, even though she's charged with these horrible murders.

There's evidence from this Janet Leach woman, who was with Dad in prison, saying he told her Mum did it with him. That's not good. I wish she wasn't giving her evidence.

There's a lot of pressure on me at the moment, especially being pregnant. I'm looking after myself and keeping myself in shape.

My life is certainly never dull. I don't know what dull means.

DAY 23—November 7

T*he prosecution called Janet Leach who, in her capacity as a "responsible adult", had spent many hours with Fred West in his prison cell. She said Fred West had told her that he would lie and take all the blame for the killings, although Rose West had played a major part.*

Mrs Leach collapsed during the lunch break, and could not complete her evidence. The court was adjourned for six days.

Stephen ...

Mum took a bashing over the evidence from Janet Leach, who said what Dad told her. I don't know why they played the tapes, where Dad admitted he's guilty, and then allowed Mrs Leach to say Dad was only saying that for the benefit of the police. It's a mistake and doesn't look good for Mum at all.

I'm quite relaxed at the moment. I've got work to keep me busy. I felt a little awkward being filmed for the documentary. There's all these people looking at you and waiting for you to say things.

I want to go and see the end of the trial. It's important for one of us to be there. I don't really get on with Mum. I've heard a lot of things about her which have left me feeling dazed and angry. But I've got to be there when it's all over.

Mae ...

When this is all over I'm definitely going away. I'm moving away from Gloucester and starting again.

REST DAY—November 9

Stephen...

I took James Weatherup and Gary Jones from *News Of The World* to the farmhouse where Dad said he tortured the victims. It's actually an old flour mill, about 20 minutes drive from Cromwell Street, down on the Severn estuary.

It's very eerie being there. I didn't believe Dad at first, but he did give me very precise directions. Dad told the police about it, and it would have come out at his trial had he lived.

I think the police will start looking there next year. I was told they won't even think of stopping until they find Mary Bastholm, whose body has vanished. They know there are more bodies, a lot more, but they don't really know how many. There's a large area to cover and I don't think they know where to start.

I know the police have gone back into the history of the place, and have looked at old photographs of the area. They told me it was empty around the times Dad was saying. But that's all they have got to go by. Until they get the imaging camera around and see if the the ground has been moved, nobody will know.

There are two great wells which have been blocked off, capped. I should think they will look in there. The police told me about them.

Nobody knows what Dad did here. He told me he did Heather at Cromwell Street, but he took the others out. He said that he tortured some of them at the mill, and they were found gagged and bound. Dad was very strong he could have easily put them in the back of the van.

When Dad confessed to me, he was really crying all the time and very vague on the detail. He was so distressed, and I didn't really want to hear it either. He admitted to me he had killed Mary Bastholm, and he also admitted it to a lot of other people. I was told he had boasted about it to the blokes in the prison in Birmingham. Apparently he was saying he had killed loads of them, but he was never going to say where they all were. A copper told me they had interviewed the inmates and that's what they had all been saying. Dad was seen with Mary before she disappeared, but no one knows where she is.

I don't know how long Dad was up at the mill for, but he did say he had bricked up a doorway when he first went there. I think I can recognise his work. It looks like one door was bricked up about 10 or 15 years ago. All the bricks bow in the middle. That's the sort of stuff he would do.

DAY 27—November 16

*O*n *Monday, November 13, Janet Leach returned to the witness stand and concluded her evidence. Under cross-examination by Richard Ferguson QC, for the defence, she admitted that in her previous evidence she had denied selling her story, whereas she had in fact entered into a book and newspaper deal worth £100,000. Mrs Leach was the last witness.*

The prosecution began its closing address that afternoon, concluding the next day. The defence's closing address occupied the whole of the following day. The judge began his summing up on Thursday, November 16.

Mae...

We went to the court today to hear the judge summing up—
me, Stephen, Stephen's friend Ian, and one of the younger
kids. It took us about two hours to drive from Gloucester to
Winchester the way Stephen drives.

Stephen arranged with Gloucester CID to get us into the
court. We parked in a multistorey car park, and the police
met us there. They drove us into the court. There were
photographers waiting outside, but because we were with
the CID they got us straight in.

We had seats in the public gallery, right over in the left
hand corner. We didn't know it, but the police weren't just
going to help us in, they were there to check on our every
movement all day long. We had two policemen assigned to
us, one sat on each side of the group, and they put Anna in
the far right hand side, quite far away.

We weren't allowed to look at her. Every time we'd lean
forward to see if she was in the gallery, the police would
lean forward as well to block the view. They'd threatened
us before, saying they'd arrest us if we even tried to speak
to her.

The judge had a morning break for ten minutes, and they
wouldn't let us go wandering around the court. Everyone
had cleared the public gallery, and they got Anna out of the
way, took her to a safe place, and then let us move. They
put us in a police room, which we weren't happy about.

They took Anna to dinner and everything. We were put in
the canteen. The police checked that we were in there, and
then brought dinner out to her.

When we were in court, Anna cried the whole way
through. Every time the family was mentioned, or she was

176

mentioned, she'd give a big sniff. If she was that upset, she shouldn't have been there.

I had butterflies, seeing the judge—apart from the fact that he looked like Santa Claus. I tried to see Mum, but the dock where she was sitting was below the public gallery. I was leaning over the balcony, but she was too far back for me to see her.

The judge was quite a frightening man. I wouldn't want to cross him. But he has got a sense of humour as well. He made a mistake, saying Mum's remains were found, not Rena's, and made everybody laugh. I think he was fair.

It seemed weird, because a lot of it I didn't know. Caroline Owens I never knew about. I thought it was a one off—they just picked her up somewhere. But she actually lived in the house, and it was quite a longer ordeal than I'd heard.

And there were things about Dad I didn't know, like the number of rapes he'd done before. I heard a bit of Dad's confession—the judge actually read his words out. Dad's English was terrible.

I must admit, some of the things he said you had to laugh at—the crudeness, and the way he said he'd raped one girl and was sick afterwards. But it was quite cold the way he said it—like he was talking about his day.

To be honest, I got a bit bored. I know they were talking about the family, but the judge took so long explaining everything, and he's got quite a dulcet tone. He pointed out every little thing, even though the jury had heard it all before.

Stephen wanted us to sit there even though we were bored. He admired what he was hearing about Dad. Not the grue- some bits, but the odd bits of humour. He looked like he wanted people to know that it was his dad they were talking about.

We weren't allowed to see Mum. We tried. In the end, we decided to leave at about 3.30. The police didn't help us at all. They said they didn't have any cars. Then they said they'd show us round the back, and we wouldn't be caught.

They showed us out this door, into the glare of all these cameras. There were four photographers flashing, and two film crews. Instead of doubling back, we just kept going. We had to walk from the court to the multistorey car park, which is about a mile, with these people following us snapping away. They were trying to get interviews, and trying to get pictures of our faces.

DAY 29—November 20

The judge concluded his summing up just before noon. The jury then retired.

Mae ...

I'm nervous. They might take ten minutes and all come back in again, or it could be days. I'm not sure if I should be sitting and just waiting. I'm trying to get on with life.

Stephen and I both saw Mum at the weekend. She's really nervous. She asked me to do her a favour, and I said what was it? Usually I can do anything for her, but this time I couldn't. She said: "What am I going to do? I don't know if I can cope, standing there, with the wait."

She wasn't sure whether they'd make her stay in prison, or in the cells under the court. In prison she could just work, polishing floors or something. But if they made her stay in the cells, ready to call her up at any time, then she's got

178

nothing to do. Sasha and Leo *(Rose's junior counsel Sasha Wass and her solicitor Leo Goatley: ed)* were going to sit with her for a bit.

Other than that, she's just got these guards with her. But it's just taking her mind off it—I don't think she can. I said, well we're in that position too. We're not sure what to do.

She said the scariest thing for her is not so much the "guilty", if she gets that, it's the fact that the judge sums up saying this person is a menace to society. She's scared he'll have a go at her.

She said she's innocent, and she's going to fight tooth and nail, and really go mad if she gets "guilty" because she really didn't do it. So she's going to appeal, she's going to write to every newspaper, she's going to make sure everybody knows. She's not going down easy.

They've put doctors on stand-by as well. She's just not sure how she'll cope. She'll probably have a heart attack.

Other inmates she was with in Durham Prison told her to have a full breakfast. They said when they had their "guilty" they didn't have breakfast, and they were starving afterwards.

Steve went to see Mum the day before me. She said she wanted to see him, desperately. She wanted to see all her children on the weekend before the verdict. Stephen went with Andrea and the twins, and they had a really good visit. It cheered her up, because she was terribly highly strung.

She feels that if it's "guilty" then she's not going to see us again. If we try to visit her, she'll refuse us. The inmate has to say "yes", so we could go but she'd just say "no". She says it's for our own good. There's no way she wants her children travelling up for the rest of her life, dragging their

179

children, to visit her. She said: "You'll have to go on as if I'd died. Try to make a life."

I must admit I can't stand going to prison. It's a horrible place. She's doing it for us, really.

DAY 30—November 21

The jury returned just before 3pm to announce the first of their verdicts: Rose West was guilty of the murders of Charmaine West and Heather West. The verdicts were unanimous. The jury returned a little over an hour later with their third unanimous verdict: guilty of the murder of Shirley Ann Robinson. They were still undecided over the murders of the other seven victims. The judge ordered them to retire overnight, and continue their discussions next day.

Stephen and Mae waited for the verdicts at a hotel near Cheltenham, with James Weatherup and Gary Jones of News of the World. Gary and James broke the news to them.

Mae...

I can't cope. Life's not worth living. It's all too much. People keep saying life is going to get better, but it isn't. It never will. I might as well take a whole load of pills. I didn't think there would be these guilty verdicts. I just didn't. I believed in Mum's innocence.

We've had everything taken away from us. It's been no life. Now I've got to bury Heather. I just don't think things are going to get any better. What's the point of making plans for the future when you don't have a life worth living. Mum won't see me again after this, that's for sure. She said she'd cut us off, and kill herself. She said she wouldn't give anyone the satisfaction of knowing she was going to be

180

inside prison for life. She'll do herself in.

I wish I knew how she was. I feel so alone. I don't know what to do. I'm pregnant and don't know how I'm going to bring the child up by myself.

I didn't dare think of guilty verdicts. I'd put it out my mind. We can forget Christmas, that's not going to happen, then there's New Year's day when Dad killed himself, so there's not going to be much of a future. God knows why we were born to suffer so much. It goes on and on, it's never ending. I'm beginning to think my child will be born handicapped. I know that's awful to think, but you do feel as if your life has been plagued.

I rang the wife of Mum's solicitor to try to make contact with him. His wife was very upset. She asked me how I was. I feel stunned, empty, and sick to the bottom of my stomach. I can't think straight.

I've been looking at a new home this afternoon. Now I don't know why I bother. Every time I try to make plans I'm smacked in the face.

Stephen ...

Mum will commit suicide, there's no way she'll want to live. She told us she didn't want any visits from us if she was found guilty. Not even from Mae. If they watch her 24 hours a day she'll still find a way to kill herself. She's got it all planned. She just won't have any will to live.

Dad did himself in for nothing. He was trying to protect her, but what was the point? He thought that, with him out the way, they would never prove anything. He said he was going to give his life for her, and he did. But what for?

Being alive makes me feel guilty. What a mess this is.

We've got nobody now. I saw Mum last Saturday and she doesn't want any contact with the family again. No letters, no calls, nothing. The jury seemed reasonable people, but I can't see how she had anything to do with Heather's death.

I think maybe she might have known and covered up for Dad. She loved him beyond the bounds of what is normal— more than someone should.

Whenever we've tried to talk to her about Dad, she won't have it. She tells me to shut up. She says she doesn't love him. But I believe she loved him more than anyone knows.

I don't buy what she's saying—I believe she's hurting for him. What would you do if someone you loved said they had lost their temper momentarily, and killed someone? You'd help them somehow, definitely.

I hope Mum gets sent back to Durham prison. She made some friends there.

All along she's had hope, hope of coming out. If she doesn't adjust, she just won't make it. I can't help thinking about what she's going through. It must be hell.

If I was with her now, I wouldn't be able to look at her because of what she must be going through. The television reports said Mum was motionless in court, and I know why. I think she was just waiting for a massive heart attack to strike her down. She had talked about that. I just know she doesn't want to go on.

God, I feel sick. Mae's in a right mess. I thought she was going into labour at one point, after the first two verdicts.

I thought it would be 50/50 if Mum got convicted but I never thought the jury would come back so quickly.

I'd love to know what they were saying in there, what points they were arguing over. She wasn't like Dad. He was ill, sick. He needed help. Mum wasn't as bad as he was. Christ, what a Christmas this is going to be. And what a New Year. That will be a year to the day when Dad killed himself.

It just gets worse. I don't know what we are going to do now.

Life has become a long line of visits to prison.

DAY 31—November 22

The jury returned just before lunch, to announce guilty verdicts on all seven remaining charges: the murders of Lucy Partington, Lynda Gough, Carol Ann Cooper, Shirley Hubbard, Therese Siegenthaler, Juanita Mott and Alison Chambers. Mr Justice Mantell imposed a life sentence for each of the ten charges. He recommended that Rosemary West should never be released.

Stephen...

You just can't prepare yourself for it. I still can't believe it, it's too final. While we were waiting for the case, there was always hope, always a chance and you could tell Mum that. Now it's just so final. It's another bit to the nightmare. We thought we had been through the worst but it just keeps going. I feel like a boxer who keeps getting up after being knocked down—I don't know why I do it.

It makes things a lot worse, having seen Mum last Saturday. I told her they didn't have the evidence to convict her and no one could be 100% sure that she was involved. She held me, cuddled me, kissed me and said: 'Thanks son, I feel a lot better now.' In a way I felt that I had let her down by saying all that. I said I promise you they won't find you 100% guilty.

We talked a lot of things out, because we hadn't been getting on that well. So we were able to remind each other that we loved each other. She said she was worried that she would be found guilty because people would want to convict somebody for these murders and now Dad's gone there was only her left to convict. She felt that might force them into it. She was very nervous, you could see it, but more placid. She wasn't cold, she was fine.

Her future is now in prison, but she said she would never last in there. She said she would make a more permanent end to it than that. But she also said that there was a life in prison and that you could build one in there. She said she would only start a new life in there if there was a chance for her to come out. She said she did not want to be found guilty and be told that she was never coming out again. She said she couldn't cope with it. Whether she has got the strength to carry on I don't know. I know she will be gutted, absolutely devastated.

It's been hard for us too. All the other families have had counselling and everything but we haven't. All they gave us was the number for Victim Support. I'm not bothered what people think of us. We've just talked about it with ourselves. I just pray to God that the police don't start digging again. I know they have got to think of the victims and the families but they have surely got to think of us sometime. We can't take any more really.

184

Mae ...

I've got to come to terms with Mum never coming out. I know that. I think Mum will adapt better to prison if she can't see us, but then if she wants us—at any time—we will be there for her.

At the moment her conviction is too final. At least before I thought there's a chance she would be found not guilty. There's still the appeal, but I don't hold out much hope. I've been campaigning for Mum for two years and was looking forward to having my mum out. I wanted Mum to be there at the birth of my child, for her to be a grand-mother. We'd made plans for it. I wanted her to be happy. She's got nobody now but herself.

Mum's solicitor told me she was shocked and devastated when she heard the verdicts. At first she didn't know what was happening, when she heard the first two verdicts, but after the third she was beginning to adjust to what was going on.

We're still making plans for the future, but not of course with Mum. We did want to move away from Gloucester-shire, but now we're not so sure. Both myself and Stephen are looking for a bigger house, but we want to keep what's left of our family together. We've got to salvage something. We have to pick up what's left of the pieces.

We have nothing, no family, no relatives, we're starting from scratch, and it's hard to accept life as it is. We've no Mum or Dad to go to if we're stuck. It's like we have no past. We've each other and that's all. It's not much.

Thank God I wasn't an only child, otherwise I don't think I'd be here now.

I don't want anyone's pity. I just wish people would leave us alone. We don't want anyone's opinion—if people said nothing that would be just fine. Leave us to pick up the bits and carry on. We don't want looks and remarks. We don't want to be reminded of what we've been through.

I know they won't let Mum go to Heather's funeral. She said about the funeral: 'If it all goes wrong, you will sort things out on your own.' We want to give Heather a decent funeral. That's something we feel very strongly about. It's time for her to be laid to rest properly.

We must have done something very wrong in an earlier life to get God doing this to us. Everybody has a few bad things happen in their lives, but nothing to what we've gone through.

I used wish Mum and Dad hadn't met and that I hadn't been born. I feel we've suffered so much. We've lost our father, now our mother, our sister, our family home and our past. It's a joke.

I feel the police and social services are to blame for letting things slip through their fingers. The police caught Dad loads of times, and if they'd sorted him out all those years ago he wouldn't have killed all those women.

Dad used to flash and pick girls up and do things to them when he was stalking them outside the Top Rank cinema, near where he used to live. But the police just moved him on without sorting the situation out.

They didn't see the signs. Dad was into everything and it was amazing the social services also didn't notice what was going on with us kids. They didn't do anything. One of Mum's clients said the kids were being abused, but they did nothing.

Stephen ...

If I had got caught with what Mum and Dad did in the seventies with that girl Caroline Owens I would have expected to be put away. But all they got was a fine. It was like a green light. You know, go for it.

I even spoke to the NSPCC when they came to the school once when I was 14 years old. Mum and Dad had worked me over one night and my girlfriend told the school, who told the NSPCC. I spoke to them a few times, but then they asked me did I want to take it any further? I said no. What did they expect me to say? I wanted them to do something about it.

Me and Mae are both looking for somewhere new to live and try and to get on with our lives. We are going to fight to get our family back together, including the ones in care. We've got to pick something up, we've lost too much. Thank God I'm not an only child and we've got each other.

Looking back, I don't think we've sat down and coped with one single bit of this. I don't think we have actually come to terms with what has happened. It happened so quick at the beginning, it was all just bang, bang, bang, like being punched around the head constantly.

I think we've been able to get through some of this by trying to keep a sense of humour. As far as I'm concerned if you can get a laugh out of something it's okay.

Dad showed me once where he met Mum at a bus stop in Cheltenham. He took me there when we were stealing bikes together. There was a whole row of bus stops and he first saw Mum when they were standing together at No. 13. Dad told me: 'That's where me and your mum met,' as we stood at the exact spot where he picked her up. I don't know why he took me there. Maybe he thought to himself this will be part of history and I should know about it.

Mae ...

He should have said to you Stephen: 'That's where I stalked your mother.' It's frightening to think that's where it all started to go wrong. It's uncanny, No. 13, who'd believe it.

There's a whole series of weird coincidences. Mum's birthday is on the 29th of November, Dad's birthday on the 29th of September and they got married on January 29th. I only realised about these dates the other day when the judge read them out in court.

Stephen ...

Numbers coming up all the time have played a big part in our lives. There was 25, Midland Road, 25, Cromwell Street, the caravan site plot number was 25, and our telephone number in Cromwell Street had the first two numbers as 25. When we went on honeymoon our chalet number was 25. It does your head in.

I do the lottery and always pick 25. If Mae goes to a hotel she won't stay in room 25. She hates the number. I know it sounds sick, but I can't get certain numbers out my head and I always think of them playing the lottery. I picked 12 last week because that's the number of bodies found. I didn't know what to choose, so I picked it. I didn't mean anything by it. We've got jack shit chance of winning. God would rather piss on us than let us win the lottery.

Appendix I
Chronology

1943: Frederick Walter Stephen West born in Much Marcle, eldest son of Mr and Mrs Walter West.

1953: Rosemary Letts born.

1956/57: Fred leaves school, barely literate.

1959: Fred is involved in a motorcycle accident which severely damages his legs and leaves him with a permanent dent in his skull.

Late 1959: Fred West is charged by police after an incident involving one of his sisters. The charges are dropped. The West family force Fred to leave home.

1961: Fred West is fined £4.00 for two counts of theft.

1962: Fred and Catherine 'Rena' Costello meet while she is working as a waitress at the New Inn at Ledbury. Rena is already pregnant by an Asian student. In November she and Fred West marry.

22nd March 1963: Charmaine Carole May West is born in Lanarkshire, Scotland. To support his family, Fred works as a milkman, ice-cream van driver and he delivers bread.

Spring, 1963: The West family moves to the Gorbals district of Glasgow.

6th July 1964: Anne-Marie West, daughter of Fred and Rena, born in Glasgow.

March 1965: Fred and Rena's first separation after a volatile

189

marriage. Fred returns to Much Marcle with Charmaine and Anne-Marie.

14th December 1965: Fred asks Hereford Social Services to put the children into care. At the time, Fred is living at a caravan site in Brockworth.

1965-1967: The marriage between Fred and Rena continues to deteriorate. Charmaine and Anne-Marie are constantly in and out of care. Anne McFall, whom Fred met in Scotland, is living with him and becomes pregnant by him.

April 1967: The last confirmed sighting of Ann McFall, aged 18. Her remains are discovered in 1994 buried in Fingerpost Field, Kempley.

1968: Fred West and Rose Letts meet at a bus stop in Cheltenham. Rose is fifteen years old and Fred is twenty-five.

1970: Rose discovers she is pregnant and that Fred West is the father. She leaves her family home to live with Fred in a flat in Cheltenham.

Feb/March 1970: Last confirmed sighting of Rena West. Her remains are discovered at Fingerpost Field, Kempley in 1994.

17th October 1970: Heather West born. Fred, Rose, Charmaine and Anne- Marie are now living at 25 Midland Road, Gloucester.

4th December 1970: Fred West imprisoned for ten months for dishonesty and theft.

Spring 1971: Last confirmed sightings of Charmaine West. Her body is discovered under the kitchen floor of 25 Midland Road. Rose and Fred tell enquirers that Charmaine had gone to live with Rena.

24th June 1971: Unconfirmed, but most likely, release date of Fred West from prison.

29th January 1972: Marriage of Fred and Rose. Fred describes himself on the marriage certificate as a bachelor.

Spring 1972: West family moves to 25 Cromwell Street.

1st June 1972: May June West, daughter of Fred and Rose, born. Later she changes her name to Mae.

Late 1972: Anne-Marie West, according to her evidence at the trial of Rosemary West, is first sexually assaulted by both Rose and Fred. She states that she was continuously abused from then until she left home.

Autumn 1972: Caroline Owens begins working for the Wests as a nanny.

November 1972: Caroline resigns, having been made uncomfortable by both Fred and Rose.

4th December 1972: Rose and Fred abduct, beat, rape and indecently assault Caroline Owens. Caroline is set free after agreeing to come back and work for them.

12th January 1973: The Wests appear at Gloucester Magistrates Court and plead guilty to charges of indecent assault and occasioning actual bodily harm. Caroline Owens is too frightened to testify against the Wests. They are fined £25 each.

March/April 1973: Last confirmed sightings of Lynda Gough. A 19-year-old seamstress, she was a regular visitor to 25 Cromwell Street and knew Fred and Rose. Her remains are found under the ground floor bathroom at 25 Cromwell Street in 1994.

November 1973: Carole Ann Cooper, a 15-year-old runaway, reported missing. Her remains are found under the cellar floor of 25 Cromwell Street in 1994.

27th December 1973: Lucy Partington, a 21-year-old student at Exeter University, vanishes from a bus stop between Cheltenham and Evesham after visiting a friend. Her remains are discovered in the cellar of 25 Cromwell Street in 1994.

3rd January 1974: Fred West goes to Gloucester Royal Hospital for treatment to lacerations on his right hand. The prosecution at the trial of Rose West assert that these injuries had probably been sustained when the body of Lucy Partington was dismembered.

26th April 1974: Therese Siegenthaler, a 21-year-old student at Woolwich Polytechnic, fails to return from a trip to Ireland and is reported missing. Her remains are found in the cellar of 25 Cromwell Street in 1994.

August 1974: Stephen West born.

14th November 1974: 15-year-old Shirley Hubbard runs away from her foster parents' home. She is never seen alive again. Her remains are found in the basement at 25 Cromwell Street in 1994.

Spring 1975: 18-year-old Juanita Mott disappears after going for an evening out in Gloucester. She had been a lodger at 25 Cromwell Street for a few months, but just before her disappearance she had moved out to live with a friend just outside Gloucester. Her remains are found in the basement of 25 Cromwell Street in 1994.

1975/1976: The exact date is unclear, but during this period the cellar floor of 25 Cromwell Street is concreted over and turned into bedrooms for the Wests' children.

April 1977: Shirley Anne Robinson, 17, comes to live at Cromwell Street as a lodger.

18th October 1977: Shirley Robinson provides a positive pregnancy test. It is general knowledge that Fred is the father. Rose is heavily pregnant at the time, but the father is not Fred.

Eyewitnesses recall Shirley behaving very affectionately with Fred, and that there was a tense atmosphere between Rose and Shirley.

December 1977: Rose gives birth to Girl A. She is of mixed race.

9th May 1978: The last confirmed sighting of Shirley Anne Robinson. She is eight months pregnant and her remains and the remains of the foetus are discovered in the garden of 25 Cromwell Street in 1994.

Autumn 1978: Girl B is born, the daughter of both Fred and Rose West .

September 1979: 17-year-old Alison Jane Chambers, who had grown up in various children's homes after the break-up of her parent's marriage, is a frequent visitor to Cromwell Street. In September 1979 she writes to her mother about a really 'homely' family which she is about to live with and work for as a nanny. She runs away from the children's home in Autumn 1979 and is never seen again. Her remains are found in the garden of 25 Cromwell Street in 1994.

1979: Anne-Marie, according to her evidence at the Rosemary West trial, is made pregnant by her father. The baby is never born.

1979: Boy C is born, the son of both Fred and Rose West.

1980: Anne-Marie leaves home and moves away from Gloucester.

1980: Eight-year-old Mae West is raped by a family friend.

1980: Girl D is born, the daughter of Rose but not Fred West. She is of mixed race.

1981: Girl E is born, the daughter of Rose but not Fred West. She is also of mixed race.

1984: Fred West starts keeping a record of Mae's menstrual cycle, as he did for all his natural daughters.

1985: Rose places advertisements in contact magazines, calling herself 'Mandy' and charging clients for sex.

17th June 1987: Heather West, aged 16, leaves school without any 'O' Levels. Increasingly under pressure to get a job, Heather finds work as a chalet maid at a Butlins camp in Devon. The job falls through the night before she is due to leave. Next day she disappears and is never seen again. Her remains are found under the patio at 25 Cromwell Street in 1994.

1988: Mae meets her first serious boyfriend, Rob Williams. After she leaves school, they move out together and buy a house with financial help from Rob's parents.

1990: Just before his 16th birthday, Stephen West is told to move out of home by his parents. They find him a bedsit nearby.

August 1992: Fred West is charged with raping a minor. Rose is charged with neglecting a child. All the younger children are taken into care.

The police begin asking detailed questions about Heather's disappearance and start a national and then international search for information concerning her whereabouts.

Fred tells Stephen and Mae that he 'had done something terrible, the worst you can ever imagine'.

Late 1992: The rape and neglect charges are dropped due to lack of evidence.

1992/1993: Mae and Stephen move back into 25 Cromwell Street to give support to their mother after the rape charges against Fred are brought and the children are taken into care.

24th February 1994: Having found no trace of Heather, the police obtain a search warrant for 25 Cromwell Street. They begin the search for her body.

The search
Day 1, Thursday, February 24th.
A team of twenty officers begin digging up the garden of 25, Cromwell Street. Gloucestershire Police refuse to explain why they are removing earth from behind the West's house. Floodlights illuminate the garden, which is hidden from view by the wall of the Seventh Day Adventist Church on one side and a high conifer hedge on the other. Police spokeswoman Hilary Allison says that they are searching 'for evidence'. A lone police officer guards the garden while sitting on a chair and reading a book through the night.

Day 2, Friday, February 25th.
Digging continues from early morning as puzzled neighbours discuss rumours surrounding the 'strange' behaviour of Fred and Rose West. Police discover small animal bones, some from chickens cooked on barbecues. Experimental electronic scanning equipment is hired from a private company to search for disturbances in the earth. The high tech gadget had been used by the Ministry of Defence to find mines in the Falklands.

  Later that day Fred and Rose West are arrested and held in separate police stations. As West is escorted away from his home he shouts to the crowd: 'I didn't kill her.'

Day 3, Saturday, February 26th.
A quarter of the 60 foot long garden has now been dug up, and four feet of top soil removed. Detectives are still inter-

viewing the Wests about Heather's disappearance. It is discovered that planning permission had not been given for a large extension on the ground floor behind the house. That night Heather's remains are dug up from the garden. Police also discover a young girl's femur bone buried near the back door.

Day 4, Sunday, February 27th.

Digging continues throughout the day and more human remains are found under the patio. Home Office pathologist Professor Bernard Knight confirms that the skeleton is that of a young girl.

Day 5, Monday, February 28th.

Fred West appears in court charged with murdering his daughter Heather between May 28th, 1987 and February 27th, 1994. He is remanded in custody to cells inside Gloucester police station. Later that night the remains of a second body, 18-year-old Shirley Robinson, are discovered in the garden. Next to her the third body, that of 15-year-old Alison Chambers, is found.

Day 6, Tuesday, March 1st.

Police acknowledge that they are dealing with one of Britain's biggest mass murder hunts. It emerges that the victims' bodies had been mutilated, and the police discover a human skull separated from the rest of the skeleton.

Day 7, Wednesday, March 2nd.

Rose West is released pending further inquiries. She is taken for her own protection to a police safe house, with her daughter Mae and son Stephen.

Day 8, Thursday, March 3rd.

Fred West collapses in court after being charged with three murders. It is revealed that Shirley Robinson was pregnant at the time of her death, and that the foetus had been removed from her womb and was found next to her. Detectives step up the search for West's first wife Catherine 'Rena' Costello, whom police had been unable to trace. By now, 200 tonnes of earth have been removed from the back garden.

Day 9, Friday, March 4th.

Police are told by West that there are further bodies inside the house. Radar equipment is brought inside to help pinpoint further bodies. The murder hunt switches to the basement.

West, who co-operated fully with police at the start of the investigation, returns to his home in the middle of the night. He is handed a can of luminous paint and he draws circles on the cellar floor where he had buried victims.

Police rip out the bath and remove the skirting board, furniture and carpets and a sink, as the search intensifies.

Day 10, Saturday, March 5th.

Detectives study further readings from the radar equipment and believe they have located another body.

Day 11, Sunday, March 6th.

The bodies of Shirley Hubbard and Lucy Katherine Partington, Kingsley Amis's niece, are found under the concrete in the cellar.

Police hint that they will soon be looking at other sites where West lived, in Midland Road, Gloucester and in Kempley, near the village of Much Marcle, on the Gloucestershire-Herefordshire border.

Officers are offered counselling to cope with the enormity of the crimes they are uncovering.

Day 12, Monday, March 7th.

The seventh body, of Juanita Mott, 17, is found in the basement. Fred West is remanded at Gloucester Magistrates' Court.

Later the eighth victim, Lynda Gough, 19, is found below West's ground floor bathroom.

Day 13, Tuesday, March 8th.

The ninth body, that of Carol Ann Cooper, 15, is found in the cellar.

Fred West is taken to the field at Kempley and then on to Cromwell Street where he stays for half-an-hour. Tonnes of concrete are poured into the cellar because digging has weakened the house, bringing it near to collapse. Officers carry five boxes of bones covered in black sheets from the house to a police van where they are taken away for forensic examination.

Day 14, Wednesday, March 9th.

Local MP Douglas French appeals to the Home Secretary for extra police funding to pay for the murder inquiry, described as Britain's biggest ever.

Day 15, Thursday, March 10th.

Frederick West is charged with five more counts of murder. Police use the scanner at the field near Kempley where they suspect more bodies will be found.

Day 16, Friday, March 11th.

Frederick West appears in court again and is remanded in custody until April 7th. Detectives suggest that West's second daughter Charmaine, from his first marriage, is buried at Midland Road, and that her mother Catherine, better known as Rena, is buried in Much Marcle.

Day 17, Saturday, March 12th

Police scale down the search to give 'exhausted and stressed' diggers at Cromwell Street a rest. Over the next two weeks police look for a suspected tenth body, but it is not found.

Day 34, Tuesday, March 29th.

Digging begins at Letterbox Field, Kempley, after West tries
to pinpoint the spot where he buried his first wife Rena, nearly
25 years ago, within sight of West's childhood home. A tent
is erected to shield the excavation work from the world's media
camped on an adjoining field. Police mount a 24-hour-a-day
guard at the site.

Day 40, Tuesday, April 5th.

Police begin digging up the front garden of 25 Cromwell Street
but nothing is found.

Day 45, Sunday, April 10th.

The remains of West's first wife Rena are finally found. Police search teams had been digging in the wrong part of the
field.

Day 55, Wednesday, April 20th.

A police diving team is called in to inspect a well which has
been discovered underneath part of the house at Cromwell
Street.

Day 61, Tuesday, April 26th.

Police switch the murder hunt to 25 Midland Road, West's
previous house.

Day 69, Wednesday, May 4th.

The remains of West's daughter Charmaine are found under
the kitchen floor at Midland Road. She is believed to have
died early in 1972, when she was eight years old.

Day 103, Tuesday, June 7th.

West's pregnant nanny Anne McFall is the last victim to be
uncovered. Her remains are found in Fingerpost Field,
Kempley, with her unborn child at her side. The 18-year-old
nursery nurse had been employed by West as a nanny and

became his lover. She met West in Glasgow where he was living with his first wife.

Now police re-open old files of unsolved sex attacks from 30 years ago, believing the serial killer could have been responsible for many more murders.

November 1994: Stephen West marries Andrea.

December 1994: Andrea gives birth to twins, a boy and a girl. The girl is named Jessica Rose West, and the boy is named Andrew Stephen West.

1st January 1995: Fred West hangs himself in his prison cell.

6th February 1995: The committal of Rose West begins. After a week-long hearing, the judge decides that she must stand trial.

3rd October 1995: The trial of Rose West begins at Winchester Crown Court.

20th November, 1995: Jury retires to consider its verdict.

21st November, 1995: After eight hours, the jury returns to find unanimously that Rose West is guilty of the murder of Charmaine West and Heather West. At this stage they are unable to reach a unanimous verdict on the other eight counts. They retire again. An hour later they return to announce their unanimous verdict that Rose West is guilty of the murder of Shirley Ann Robinson. As they are still undecided on the other seven counts, they retire to their hotel overnight.

22nd November 1995: Shortly before lunch, the jury returns a guilty verdict on all seven remaining counts. The judge imposes ten life sentences, one for each of the murders. Rosemary West should never be released, he says.

Appendix II
Letters from prison

Fred and Rosemary West both wrote letters to Stephen and Mae from prison. Fred West's letters are mostly addressed to Stephen. Rose West's letters are mostly addressed to Mae. As the younger children are subject to a care order and cannot be named, we have substituted ('Girl A'), ('Boy C') and so on for their names in the text that follows.

Fred West's Letters

1
To Stephen & andrea
I got your photos of you wedding thy ar Beautiful son. andrea and May looks stunning you wer or Write. HA, HA, son have you seen ('Girl A') and hur babys son if you see them give them all my love I got the batteries and tobacco and £20 thankyou son. have you sent your mum photos of your Wedding I beat andrea is getting very bige it is 2 babys or moor HAHA that my Boy, get may to Write me I hame allways thinking of you all. I may be in High Court in London to give evidence against Mr Ogden in December.
Gave My love to
andrea,
Love Dad xxx
PS My Book is cuming on Well tell you moor about it When I see you have you and May dun your, the Books called
(I Was loved By an angel)

2
To Stephen & andrea
Watt you Boy I have not herd from you have you seen May or
Rose or ('Girl A') have you got a car of van, how is andrea
getting on with the Babys is she Having problems With her
pregnant How far pregnant is she a Boy and a Girl Wood be nice
have you got names for them, how ar you gating on With Derek
as he still got cowboy Working for him, can you send me sum
Batteries R6 and sum tobacco When you can have you seen ('Girl
A') Baby anna cam to see me and Janet, I Wood love may to
Write to me May nows about Rose, I Was her true friend never
mind I have got you and ('Girl A'), I Wish andrea all the Best and
send my love to her see you soon, all my love DAD

3
To Stepen and andrea
Hi Stev long time no see have you forgot your DAD I have not
heard from you FOR a long time 4 week I sent you a letter, ann
has cum to see me 2. Janet is cuming to see me 1 A week so
cume and see me soon I have lots to tell you a bout Mr Ogden.
Janet got me a new solicitors My new one ar Bobbetts Mackan
20A Berkeley Square Clifton Bristol BS8 1HP Telephone 0272,
299001 Mr TONY Miles, send in tobacco, My new Solicitors
dont send in tobacco. I have got all My thing back the fish ar at
Mr Ogden. Office annd is going have them for the Girls she Will
hav to Get them dont till Rose or May.
all my love DAD
see you soon SON

4

To stephen - andrea

you Wer not in court on thursday it Went Well, My new Solicitors brilliant he sorted that court out Rose Luckd Well, is MAy seeing Rose tell May to Write to me. I did not see Anna in court to see Janet. Well congratulate on twins first time thats one up on your Dad dont mack a habit of it babys cost Money lots of Money Make shor you love them. and your Wife, dont spend all your Time at Work. I did that and luck What went on at home. Money is not everything your home and family is. Well congratulation on pasting your driving test the first time have you told the Police. I had a vist from Janet on friday morning anna is cuming to see me see you soon all my love DAD.

give you a x from me

Stevphen tell May to tell Rose the thing anna has is for Me so no one sell it, it Will be sorted out after the court case Mr Ogden was going to keep it for me but he Was going to sell it, tell May I love and I Wont her to cume and see me or Write to me I Will Write to her if she sends me her address or PHONE number I Will ring her it Will be after 700 till 830 at night, a buout the fish no one Wanted them so Way cant Carol and Michelle May loves anna Michelle and Carol I no that and May no it to, it time all of you got to gather and protect your own brother and sisters that all you got of your pased, so Boy see May and tell her to stop I love you all. Rose is Bracking you up and you all helping Rose to do it Rose love Rose not you lot. You no that.

5

To Stephen and andrea
Hi Boy you lette me down on satday it you cant cume to see me
Ring the Prison and say you cant Make it. it makes it look bad on
me. so please Boy ring in, hows andrea gitting on with the Babys
its not long be for she will have them I did not see you in court
have you seen May When you do tell her dad love her and tell
her to Write to me or cum and see me do you no mum is going
for a Oldstill trial so she cud get out of it cud you send me sum
moor tobacco and Batteries in When you can, do you see ('Girl
A') if you do tell her to write to Dad and tell me all a bout her son
and her and give her a kiss and cuddle from dad Will Love you
Boy give andrea My love and tell her it not long now be for she
Will have the babys to play With. Well Boy Write soon or cum
and see me
all my love to you
and andrea
all Ways in my thoughts Dad.

6

To my Boy Stephen
I no you love your DAD he loved you I have a new Solicitors
Bobbetts Mackan I have a team of 7.
have you seen May tell her, dad wood lick to see her I ham her
DAD and I love her. but she no that I forgive her for watt she
said to THE police a bout me but I no Rose did that. cume and
see me soon. (Two sentences removed on legal grounds.) I
Wanted to tell the truth give my love to May tell her to cum and
see me soon.x
give my love to   love DAD
ANDREAx

7

To Stephen and Andrea

Watts going on With May and anna and Rose I was told by Mr
OGDEN that Rose approve of ('Girl A'), had Watt she wonted
and to sell watt left and have the money to help her out so watt as
anna got, When are you coming to see me bring andrea with you
cum soon son, alot has hapend since I saw you last I have a new
barrister, I get on With him My case is in a mess. have you seen
May tell her dad love her and give her a x from dad   all my love
to
Stephen and andrea
see you soon DAD xx
I have got tobacco
I need R6 battery get Rayovac VIDOR Longer Life alkaline

8

To may West

Hi May it your Dad Writeing to you. or lette me have your
telephone number I can phone you at night from 700 to 800 or
Write to me as soon you can, please may I have to sort out watt
Mr Ogden did to me, my new solicitors are Brilliant I Read What
you sead about me in News of the   that was loylty you read
watt Scott canavan sead He had 1 day training 3 weeks be for. ar
you Working Stevphen sead you have a car Watt is it, about anna
I now Watt anna is doing I Will sort that out I gave the fish to
Michelle and carol, the Bar is in storage I did not no your address, Steven was on honeymoon, that how anna got to no about
it I did not no anna had thing from Cromwell ST you or Stevphen
nos about Watt see wonted I was told Rose sed yes to ('Girl A')
having it, I have not herd Watt Rose Wanted to do With the
House I have been told By my solicitors not to sell it Till after the
court, Give, ('Girl A'), my Love and her Baby Boys May Dad
love you We had go time   all I Love and x
Dad

9

Hi son

I got your letter and the batteries and tobaco. I ham sorry to hear that andrea has been in hospital there no need to cum to see me you need to stay with andrea, she needs all the help you can give hur. andrea cane go in to premature labour or labour at anytime so you need to be with her son and When she has the babys no Working all day and night like I did or you cud end up in hear, all ways no What going on in your home pliase son all Ways spend as much time With your Wife and children as you can and love your Wife and children, there the most valuable thing you will ever have in your life so look after it son, When you see May or ('Girl A') tell them to Write to me and tell them I love them. so pliase son look after andrea and tell her it will be all worth it give my love to andrea,

I Will be all Ways thinking of you
all my love son
Dad

10

To stephen and andrea

Will Boy Been a father is not so easy is it, but the babys Will make it all Worth it Will Boy I was allways on to about Been to hard on your girl friends by wonting to no what they were doing all the time Will you got it right I had it Wrong look What your Mother Was up, you were telling me to sort her out or throw her out, and you Wood not have a Wife like her. but not one of you told me What was going on at home. if I hade not Work all day and night I did What I thought was right for you all. Well that enough of my problems just mack shor andrea gets all the help she wonts but remember a mother nose her baby Best, and dont you work all day and night spend has much time as you can With

your children by the time you get this letter you will be a dad
gave my love to andrea and all my Best Wishes to her and tell
andrea it Will be Worth it all I Will be thinking of you all
all my love Dad.
to ('GIRL A')
Well ('Girl A') your baby son is Beautiful just like you darling
pleas look after my grandson allways be With him tell him is
grampy love him and give him a big kiss and cuddle for me,
thank you ('Girl A') for the PHOTOS of you and ('Boy F'). it Will
take me about twelve to eighteen month Well ('Girl A') you no
your Dad as never harm anyone I loved you all and that May and
I will Write to you soon
all my thoughts ar With you
('Girl A'), love Dad.xxxxxxxx
(a big x) FOR ('Boy F')

Rosemary West's Letters

1
Hi Mae,
How are things with you? I don't realy know what to write about,
as these letters seem to take so long getting to you. I was writing
in my diary, and it came to me that I hav'nt told you to much
latly, how much I love you. So hears my feeble attempt:-

I love you like a part of myself,
I love you like the dawn,
I love you like the moon & stars,
And the sun on a summer's morn.

I love you like the birds and bee's
I love you like flower's sweet,
I love you like deep blue sea's,
And memories dear to keep.

I love you like your made of glass
I love you like your gold,
I love you like the rarest diamond
To precious to be sold.

In all seriousness though, you are very precious indeed, and it's
not only me who thinks so. I'm very proud of you, you realy are
a wonderfull person.

Love you allway's
Mum   xxxxx   xxxx

2
Hi Darling,
Thought I would drop you a line and tell you I love you, and how
much I realy enjoyed your visit. It's just great chatting to you,
and you leave me with a wonderfull feeling of warmth and
security. You not only tolerate me, but believe in me too! You are
very special to me. I hope you had a nice break in London, but of
course you did. Being close to the one you love makes the world
a much better place. I can't tell you just how happy it makes me
to know you have someone for whom you care so much. He's a
lovly person.
      There's a lovly song they play on the radio, it's called You
Don't Know, sung by Helen Shapiro, I think it's very apt. Every
now and then they play a piece of music from Wathering Hieghts.
It's called Tara's Theme, it's beautiful and I allway's think of you
know who. Who's going soft then. Thanks for the poster, it's
great and I'v put it up on my pin board. So now I can show you
off. I was wondering, if you could give Barb's? address, she's a
loving person, and we have been good friends in the past. I
thought I might write to her and let her know I'm O.K. I'll leave
you now, take care of yourself.

208

love as allway's
Mum
xxxxx
xxxx
P.S. Has Steve sent a card.

3
Sunday,
Dear Steve and Andrea,
I can't tell you how wonderfull it was to see you both on Saturday. You both looked well, and I hope you look after yourselvs
all the time. I'v just realised that I don't have your address, so
you will have to send it to me sometime. It's been a lovly day
here today. I have a nice view from my window. You want to see
the sky sometimes, beautifull colours. Sometimes the clouds are
white and fluffy again'st a clear bright blue sky. We have a air-
base here nearby. We get allsorts of aircraft come over. The other
day a micro-light was hoovering around the sky. Sometimes you
get a loud, drawing noise and a jet will whiz overhead. Or a
wrilling sound and it will be three choppers. It's surprissing what
comes over here. One day it was the 'Red Arrows', we've had
plenty of air ballons, come right close over the rooftops. I could
see the people quite clearly in the baskets. Or you get jets making
patterns, again'st the sky. Nice when you've got time to look out
your window! To my great surprise, the teacher's came up the
other day, I stood there with my mouth open for a couple of
minute's, wondering what to say. Then they asked me daft
questions like, Would you like to learn a language like Hungarian
or German! Someone wrote to me saying, 'think how proud the
Grand children will be when Granny gets a P.H.D. for nucelar
phisic's'.
   What a laugh. Crumbs, granny! old age crepping up on me. But
I like the game's of table-tennis and badmington when I go to the

gym, but one of the gym teacher's makes me do five miles on the exercise bike as-well. But we do get a lovly shower afterward's.

There was some babies clothes at home. but I don't know what's happened to them. I don't know if you could make use of them, if you could find them. And there was some other stuff that might be usefull if you wanted. Have you been through it all? There's been some great music on the radio today. I'v been quite happy now I'v got things to do. Well my darling's, I will leave you now and go to bed. Once again, Thanks for coming, I know how difficult it is, when you have so much to do. At least you know where to find me!

Lots of Love and Kisses.

Mum xxxxxxxx

4

Sunday 19th June.

Hello Darling,

Thanks for my cigarette's and your letter. Mae, what you do is your business, I'm just pleased you have someone, and that they care for you so much. Like our friend say's, your a very level-headed person, I'm sure you can make your own decisions. As long as your happy, that's all that matters.

I was so pleased to hear that ('Girl A') has had her baby and that everything's allright. You can tell me all about it, when I see you next. And at least you know now, that it's a boy you have to buy for. I wondered why I was so restless last night. I woke up at 2 o'clock, and tried to make out why. I tossed and turned for a bit, and then went back to sleep. An hour later I'm awake again this time with stomach ache. By the time the mornings got here, I'v got stomach and back ache, and even my legs ached. But then again I could of just had a bad night and I'm blaming it on poor old ('Girl A')! I know the time because I have the radio on in bed at night. I put the ear-phone in, and I even fall asleep with it still

210

switched on. I listen to radio 2 all day and then turn it to the oldies station at night. I think I'm a bit old-fashioned. Well I'll get this terribly bad spelt letter of to you, and you can have a jolly good laugh about it. I would of, wrote it all over again, but I just can't be bothered.

Love you so much,

Mum.

xxxx

xxxx

P.S. Send EMMA my love.

5

MONDAY 6th JUNE,

My dear Mae,

Hope this letter finds you well and happy. I'm settling in OK, and I'm keeping fit and occupied. English lessons are under way and I hope to learn how to spell a lot better. I go to the Gym every-day, sometimes before breakfast. Sofar I'v had a go at Badmington yesterday and table-tennis today. Couldn't imagine me playing games, could you? How's Steve. You can tell me what you've been doing as well. And not to forget about ('Girl A'), and how thing's are with her. The weather's not been to good here, only a few hour's of sunshine, but the birds love it when it does arrive. I have a wall outside one of my window's, and the pidgeon's have been using it to mate on. They get feed from the canteen, so there's lots of fat one's about.

When you write would you give me Steve's full address and phone number, if he has one. I'm reading a book called 'THE SHELL SEEKERS' it realy is good. It's all about a painting and the family that own's it. I'v got loads more to read and I hope their as good as the one's I'v allready read. Mae, I need money to buy thing's with, but it has to be sent by post. If you can send me 3 five pound notes in an envalope plus 40 Silk Cut, I would be

211

very gratefull. Make sure the Envalope has my number, name and address on it. I'm sorry love, I forgot to tell you, that you maybe searched when you come to see me. Just so that you know. Have you got access to a garden where you live? It would be nice for you to have somewhere to sit out in the sun, and maybe even to hang your washing out in the fresh air. It dries so quick in the nice weather, and smells realy fresh. I'll leave you now, and send this letter on.

Love you allway's

Mum

xxxx   xxxxx

6

WEDNESDAY

Hi Darling,

I thought I would drop you a few lines just to apologise. I felt I was insensitive and rather rash on Tuesday. I might even say I was being a tiny bit selfish.

  Please thank ('Girl A') for my watch and tell her Mum will allway's treasure it. Tell her I will write to her as soon as I can get things sorted out with Social Services.

  I'v been to the gym this-morning. We have two new computer-ised rowing machines. They cost a bomb! Thier good though, it's a sort of all-in-one exercise machine. The teachers realy excited about them.

  Thank you for my fags, in fact thanks for everything you do for me. I hope I will never take you for granted. I can't tell you how wonderfull it is to know that I am loved no-matter what sort of dreadfull situation I might find myself in.

Remember I will love you allways.

Mum.   xxxxx xxxxx

7

My dearest Mae,

Well here I'am, settling down in a new place. It's very nice here
and everyone is being so good to me. How are things with you? I
was so pleased to see you Tuesday. I know how hard it was for
you, and how nither of us said half the things we wanted to.
Visiting should be much easier for you here. You can come
anytime, as I'm allowed visit's every day. I just can't wait to see
you, and have a good chin wag! It will be good to see Steve too!
as I hav'nt seen him for a long time. I can't tell you how much I
appreciate you being there for me. Did you have a good birthday.
I do hope you didn't have to work that day. You know you said
you didn't like the sound of key's rattling, well they don't rattle
here, they jingle like the sound of bells on father christmas's
raindeer. If this letter get's to you before Tuesday would you
bring down with you, a very small radio and the batteries for it.
They have to be DURACELL.

DONT bring cloths?, I don't need them yet. Guess what, I'm
smoking tobacco, that's all I can afford. But it does'nt matter, I'm
quite happy, as long as I can see you. You and Steve can write to
me as well, if you have time. I'll leave you now and get this letter
on it's way.

Love you so much,

Mum

xxxx

xxxxx

P.S. send Steve my love.

8

FRIDAY 10th JUNE

My dear Mae,

It realy was wonderful to see you. I still didn't tell you all I
wanted to. So please come again soon, I realy do miss you to talk

213

to. I love you, and there's no one I trust more.Thanks for my radio, It's great to have it back. I recieved the money, but I did ask Steve to put a letter in with the money and said that he had sent them, but they didn't get here, do you know why? I can have them, but they have to be sent in by post. Oh it's allright, they've just got here. Ignore what I'v just said! I still need time to work out how things are done here, I'll learn, slow, but I'll learn. By what you've told me, sometimes I think I'm the lucky one to be here away from all the shit. You realy are a very strong person, and you are a constant source of comfort and delight in my life.

Started a new book last night, It's called 'THE PRINCE OF TIDES'. It's got realy big words, so I asked for a dictionary. It's flippin massive.

Well darling, It's bedtime, so I'll snuggle down. I hope you can make sense of my letters. Give Baggy? a kiss for me. Can't wait to see you again.

Lots of Love
Mum
xxxxx
xxxx